beyond today

beyond today

WORDS

OF WISDOM

FOR THE

ROAD AHEAD

Beyond Today

Copyright © 2000 by Good News Publishers

Published by Crossway Books
        a division of Good News Publishers
        1300 Crescent Street
        Wheaton, Illinois 60187

Unless otherwise identified, Scripture is taken from the *Holy Bible: New International Version*® Copyright © 1973, 1978, 1984 by International Bible Society. Used by permission of Zondervan Publishing House. All rights reserved.

The "NIV" and "New International Version" trademarks are registered in the United States Patent and Trademark Office by International Bible Society. Use of either trademark requires the permission of International Bible Society.

Scripture quotations taken from the *Revised Standard Version* are identified RSV. Copyright © 1946, 1953 1971, 1973 by the Division of Christian Education of the National Council of the Churches of Christ in the U.S.A.

Scripture quotations marked NASB are taken from the *New American Standard Bible*® Copyright © The Lockman Foundation 1960, 1962, 1963, 1968, 1971, 1972, 1973, 1975, 1977, 1995. Used by permission.

Scripture references marked NKJV are taken from the *New King James Version.* Copyright © 1982, Thomas Nelson, Inc. Used by permission.

Scripture references marked NEB are taken from *The New English Bible* © The Delegates of the Oxford University Press and The Syndics of the Cambridge University Press, 1961, 1970.

Scripture references marked KJV are taken from the King James Version.

Scripture references marked NLT are taken from the *Holy Bible, New Living Translation*, copyright © 1996. Used by permission of Tyndale House Publishers, Inc., Wheaton, Ill. 60189. All rights reserved.

Book design: Cindy Kiple

First printing 2000

Printed in the United States of America

LIBRARY OF CONGRESS CATALOGING-IN-PUBLICATION DATA
Beyond today : words of wisdom for the road ahead.
    p.   cm.
  ISBN 1-58134-170-9 (hc : alk. paper)
  1. High school graduates—Religious life—Quotations. 2. College graduates—Religious life—Quotations. 3. High school graduates—Conduct of life—Quotations. 4. College graduates—Conduct of life—Quotations. 5. Christian life—Quotations, maxims, etc. I. Crossway Books.
BV4529.2 B49 2000
248.8'34—dc21

                               00-023576
                               CIP

15	14	13	12	11	10	09	08	07	06	05	04	03	02	01	00
15	14	13	12	11	10	9	8	7	6	5	4	3	2	1	

contents

hat does the Lord require of you?
To act justly and to love mercy and
to walk humbly with your God.

MICAH 6 : 8

Purpose and Priorities

A SANCTIFIED LIFE

IS SIMPLY ONE

THAT HAS BEEN

SET APART FOR

GOD'S PURPOSES.

Donna Morley

As the old saying goes, "If you aim

at nothing, you will surely hit it." But at what targeted goals should the

believer take aim?

Your daily planner may be a sophisticated tool for helping you

manage your many "To Do" lists, but as believers we have a living, per-

sonal Word from God that can provide us with not only "To Do" sug-

gestions to shape our priorities, but with "To Be" instructions that

definitively outline why God created us.

Let the timeless words of Scripture and the encouragement of

fellow believers spur you toward understanding the purposes and

priorities God has chosen for you.

It is for freedom that Christ has set us free. Stand firm, then, and do not let yourselves be burdened again by a yoke of slavery.

Galatians 5:1

If your priority is to exalt Christ in every circumstance, whatever furthers that purpose will bring you joy.

John MacArthur

When a man isn't a Christian, he is trying to live in a universe that isn't there. There is a truth in the universe, and when we accept Christ as our Savior, when we bow before the God who is there, we obey the truth of God, which is also the truth of the universe.

Francis A. Schaeffer

What is my goal? What is my chief end? It is essential to recognize that I am created in the image of God for the purpose of reflecting His image. Sin marred that image, but through the life, death, and resurrection of Jesus Christ that image can be restored. Sovereign grace regenerates me so that I can believe and empowers me so that I can reflect the image of God.

Susan Hunt

Do you want to love God? Then give Him primacy, focus on His person, reverence Him with your words, and invest your time with Him. As a result, you will grow more and more to live out life's highest priority—loving God with your all! Your life will then be a sweet aroma to Him.

R . K e n t   H u g h e s

When your passion upon getting up each morning is to say, "How can I make God look good today?"; when the passion of your life is to someday open your eyes in eternity and hear Jesus say, "Well done, My good and faithful servant"; when that becomes the consuming passion of your existence, it absolutely transforms your everyday experience.

T o n y   E v a n s

Know that the LORD is God. It is he who made us, and we are his; we are his people, the sheep of his pasture.

P s a l m   1 0 0 : 3

Every divine precept is "right." It shows you the path that is right and true. What a wonderful confidence that is! While many around you may be discouraged or despondent because of their

lack of direction and purpose, God's Word is a lamp to your feet and a light to your path (Psalm 119:105). It guides you through the difficult mazes of life and gives your life eternal significance. Don't live simply for your own pleasures. Your life has a high and holy purpose, and each day can be filled with joy as you see that purpose unfold.

John MacArthur

He made us and understands us, and we must trust Him to accomplish His purposes for our lives.

Sheila Cragg

His plans and purposes for us are for our good. And if we are sincerely willing to learn from our Good Shepherd, choosing to believe and obey His precepts, commandments, and instructions, we will find His burden light and His yoke easy.

Debra Evans

But be sure to fear the LORD and serve him faithfully with all your heart; consider what great things he has done for you.

1 Samuel 12:24

*A*n airplane is meant to fly, a car is built to be driven, and clothes are designed to be worn. You would have very little use for a plane that would not fly, a car that would not move, or clothes that can no longer be worn.

Why? Because their purpose is not being realized. It's a great frustration to have things that are no longer useful. God must feel that way about us sometimes.

You were designed to know Him, not simply to have a comfortable life. You were not created just to get married, have children and a successful career, then grow old and enjoy retirement. These are some of life's benefits, its side dishes, not its purpose.

The tragedy today is that we have taken life's benefits and tried to make them our purpose. We're trying to make the side dishes the main course. The result is that we often find the benefits very unsatisfactory. No wonder.

So if the purpose of life is not marriage, success, happiness, or any of that, what is it? What were we created for? We were created to know and worship God with an all-consuming passion. That's it. That's why Paul tells us to do everything to God's glory (1 Corinthians 10:31).

Bringing glory to something means to put it on the mantel where it can be admired. A woman seeks glory when she decorates her home in such a way that guests say, "Wow, where did you get that?" She puts a special treasure on display so that when people see it, they are in awe.

That's what we're supposed to do for God. We're supposed to display Him in such a way that people are awed by Him. Glorifying God means to make Him look good, to place Him on display so that when others see our lives, they are in awe of our God.

Even in the everyday stuff, your goal should be to make God look good. But I can tell you, it takes real passion to live like that.

TONY EVANS

He asked him, "Of all the commandments, which is the most important?"

"The most important one," answered Jesus, "is this: 'Hear, O Israel, the Lord our God, the Lord is one. Love the Lord your God with all your heart and with all your soul and with all your mind and with all your strength.' The second is this: 'Love your neighbor as yourself.' There is no commandment greater than these."

Mark 12:28-31

You are one of God's lights in a sin-darkened world, and while most people will reject Christ, others will be drawn to Him by the testimony of your life. Be faithful to Him today so He can use you that way.

John MacArthur

This is why God made us in the first place: He made us for His glory (Isaiah 43:7). "What is the chief end of man?" asks the first question of the Westminster Shorter Catechism. It is a question about the ultimate meaning of human existence. What is life all about? The answer is: "Man's chief end is to glorify God, and to enjoy him forever." That is a good answer, maybe even the best answer.

Philip Graham Ryken

The fundamental commandment, first in importance as well as in order, and basic to every other, is, "You shall have no other gods before me." True religion starts with this as one's rule of life.

Your god is what you love, seek, worship, serve, and allow to control you. Paul calls covetousness "idolatry" (Colossians 3:5) because what you covet—houses, possessions, ornaments, money, status, success, or whatever—is "had" as a god in this sense. To have your Maker and Savior as your God in preference to any other object of devotion (which is the point of "before") means that you live for Him as His person in faithful and loyal obedience. The attitude of devoted loyalty to God, expressed in worship and service according to His Word, is that fear of the Lord (reverence, not panic!) which the Bible sees as the beginning and indeed the essence of wisdom (Job 28:28; Psalm 111:10; Proverbs 1:7; 9:10). Heart-loyalty is the soil out of which holy living grows.

J. I. Packer

Our responsibility is to represent God as tactfully as we can because we are messengers of peace. Our daily briefing on God's plan for the world comes through the time we spend in His Word. We represent the King of kings, and our homes are embassies. What a privileged position we hold!

Ellen Banks Elwell

Since, then, you have been raised with Christ, set your hearts on things above, where Christ is seated at the right hand of God. Set your minds on things above, not on earthly things. For you died, and your life is now hidden with Christ in God.

Colossians 3:1-3

We can exalt diet over duty, dress over devotion, work over witness, music over motive, form over function—the list is endless. Instead, may we put God first, and demonstrate that by consistently spending time with Him in His Word and in prayer.

Tom Elliff

Therefore, I urge you, brothers, in view of God's mercy, to offer your bodies as living sacrifices, holy and pleasing to God—this is your spiritual act of worship.

Romans 12:1

Perhaps the most common thing given priority over God is self. There are many today who worship themselves with all their heart and strength and serve only themselves.

R. Kent Hughes

Those who love God shun worldliness, pursue righteousness, and know the satisfaction that comes from pleasing Him. That's the essence of the Sermon on the Mount: "Seek first His kingdom, and His righteousness; and all [you need] shall be added to you" (Matthew 6:33 NASB). Keep that goal uppermost in your mind as you face the challenge of each new day.

John MacArthur

Why bother to ask God to bless us unless our priorities are conscientiously aligned with His? That will affect our conduct and speech, our pocketbooks and our imaginations, our vocation and our retirement, where we live and what we do and how we do it.

D. A. Carson

You were redeemed to glorify God through righteous deeds. Make that your priority today.

John MacArthur

Possession of material goods has to be one of the areas for individual, thoughtful choice. A bigger and nicer home has its benefits, of course, but is it worth so much juggling of time and energy that there is never enough left for abundant life . . . ?

Susan Schaeffer Macaulay

Why don't people prize and pursue the pearl of wisdom above everything else? The reason is that the gaining of wisdom requires the total sacrifice of our single most precious possession: ourselves. More specifically, what is required is the surrender of our wills.

Mike Mason

Come, let us bow down in worship, let us kneel before the LORD our Maker; for he is our God and we are the people of his pasture, the flock under his care.

Psalm 95:6-7

It is essential to keep our hearts burning brightly with love for Him, because our hearts will love something. . . . We must let our fears go and allow Him to love us. He is a gracious God, and His ways are good. We can trust Him with our hearts. Paul encouraged the younger Timothy: "Fan into flames the spiritual gift God gave you when I laid my hands on you. For God has not given us a spirit of fear and timidity, but of power, love, and self-discipline" (2 Timothy 1:6-7 NLT).

Nancie Carmichael

or I know the plans I have for you," declares the LORD, "plans to prosper you and not to harm you, plans to give you hope and a future. Then you will call upon me and come and pray to me, and I will listen to you. You will seek me and find me when you seek me with all your heart."

JEREMIAH 29:11-13

Guidance and God's Will

CAN YOU KNOW

GOD'S WILL

FOR YOUR LIFE?

THANK GOD, THE

ANSWER IS YES!

Ray Pritchard

At each bend in the road, you peer

ahead, longing to see where Christ is taking you. How can you make

sure you're on the path God's chosen for you? How can you be sure the

plans and decisions you're making are in His will?

God's Word holds the key—and the assurance that God is able to

get you where He wants you to go. ❧

God wants you to know His will more than you want to know it, and therefore He takes personal responsibility to see that you discover it. Knowing God's will is ultimately God's problem, not yours. The sooner you realize it, the happier you will be. Too many people agonize over God's will as if God were playing a cosmic game of hide and seek. The entire Bible teaches us the opposite, that our God seeks us. He continually takes the initiative to reveal Himself to us. Therefore, knowing God's will is simply a subsection of the larger question of knowing God personally.

Ray Pritchard

The leading of the Spirit follows in the footsteps of Jesus. If you are going where Jesus would not go, doing what Jesus would not do, saying what Jesus would not say (write this down in ink; carve it in granite), He is not the one leading you.

To follow Him is to follow His example. To be led by Him is to follow His Word, to keep His commandments. If we know that the Spirit does not lead us to disobey, to sin, or to do what is contradictory to His Word, then we also know that the Spirit does lead us to obey, to avoid sin, and to do what we are instructed to do in His Word.

David Haney

uidance comes through obedience in the ordinary. . . . 99 percent of life is ordinary. It's just the same old stuff day after day. You get up in the morning, take a shower, put your clothes on, eat breakfast, get the kids ready for school, go to work, hope the kids are OK, come back from work dead-tired, read the paper, watch TV, try to be nice, eat supper, play with the kids, flop into bed dead-tired, then get up the next morning and do it all over again. That's the way life is. It's the same old thing day after day.

Where do you begin discovering the will of God? You begin by doing what you already know to be the will of God in your present situation. So many of us live for those mountain-peak experiences, those times when the clouds part and God seems so close to us.

Many people wish those spectacular moments would happen every day. Often when we say, "God, show me Your will," what we really mean is, "Lord, give me some feeling, some insight, some spiritual revelation." And God says, "I have already shown you My will. Now, just get up and do it!" . . .

You discover God's will in the nitty-gritty of the valley of every single day. The Bible says, "Whatever your hand finds to do, do it with all your might" (Ecclesiastes 9:10). Why should God show you His will for the future if you aren't doing the will of God in the present?

RAY PRITCHARD

Spending time in God's Word and opening our hearts to His truth will guide us in our choices to take paths that are straight, not crooked.

Ellen Banks Elwell

God gives Christians His light not simply so they may have it, but so they may live by it. The psalmist affirms, "Thy word is a lamp to my feet, and a light to my path" (Psalm 119:105 NASB).

John MacArthur

Since you are my rock and my fortress, for the sake of your name lead and guide me.

Psalm 31:3

It is very easy and tempting to make choices based only on what we see or what is readily available. How much harder, but wiser, to seek and follow God's wisdom about a significant choice.

Ellen Banks Elwell

I will instruct you and teach you in the way you should go; I will counsel you and watch over you.

Psalm 32:8

beyond
today

There's the story of a pilot who came on the loudspeaker mid-flight
and said, "I have some good news and some bad news. The bad
news is, we've lost all our instrumentation and don't know where
we are. The good news is, we have a strong tailwind and are making great time." That's an accurate picture of how many people live:
They have no direction in life, but they're getting there fast!

We as Christians are to be different because we have divine
guidance and eternal goals. Our lives are to be marked by a confident trust in God and a pursuit of spiritual excellence.

John MacArthur

When you and I want direction for our lives, we may not always
be clear about it or certain that the direction has been given—even
when we get it. That's not always because of weak faith. That may
be just our human inability to know what God knows. God sees
our tomorrows; we don't. Years of experience have taught me that
God will probably leave me alone if I'm on the right path, but He
will give me a good shove in the right direction if I'm not.

Roger C. Palms

When the Lord indicates that we should wait for further guidance,
it is imperative to follow the advice of Proverbs 3:5-6 (NKJV):

Guidance and God's Will

"Trust in the LORD with all your heart, and lean not on your own understanding. In all your ways acknowledge Him, and He shall direct your paths." Through prayer and the study of God's Word, we can seek the mind of God. A reluctance to discover His will indicates either an exaggerated self-confidence or the fear that God will not endorse our selfish desires.

Tom Elliff

It is through the act of obeying God that adults and children follow a safe, definite path that leads to the liberty of green pastures and still waters for the soul and in actual life too. If we listen to the words of God, we never ignore His directions. We are to listen, understand, and take His offer of forgiveness to heart. We bow before the Creator, and a desire to follow and obey will increase as we stumble along. God's rules and ways *are* the way of life. His way followed is a gift, not a test.

Susan Schaeffer Macaulay

If any of you lacks wisdom, he should ask God, who gives generously to all without finding fault, and it will be given to him. But when he asks, he must believe and not doubt, because he who doubts is like a wave of the sea, blown and tossed by the wind.

James 1:5-6

Three times . . . David prays for guidance [in Psalm 143]. Each petition has a slightly different focus. "Show me the way I should go"
(143:8) reflects David's confusion, but also hints that there are
unique and individual elements to the guidance he needs. . . .
"Teach me to do your will" (143:10) now focuses entirely on God's
agenda ("for you are my God"). Knowing and doing God's will is
the very stuff of guidance. "May your good Spirit lead me on level
ground" (143:10) is to admit that we may trip as well as rebel,
stumble as well as stray—and always we need help.

D . A . C a r s o n

Look back over the pathways of your life.

Where have you come from?

Do you see the shepherding of God in your life?

Can you spot His fingerprints on your decisions and provisions?

All those who are His children can. . . . The child of God can see
the evidence in his life of God's transforming care. This is how we
know the Spirit of God has been and is guiding us.

D a v i d H a n e y

God tells us to cease striving and know that He is God (Psalm
46:10). We can be calm because God is on the throne. He sover-

eignly controls all things in our lives, and His providence guides us (Psalm 48:14).

Donna Morley

It is hard to pray, "Your will be done" because we often doubt that God wants the best for us. . . . It's hard to pray that prayer because it means giving up control of your life. But that doesn't mean your life will go out of control. It just means that your life is surrendered to God's control.

Ray Pritchard

Doing God's will, action based on God's teaching, will follow after a person meditates—hour by hour, day by day, year by year— upon that which God has carefully given and protected so that it might be available to anyone.

Edith Schaeffer

Seeking God is more than having a casual interest in Him. It's similar to going on a hunt, and the place for us to start is God's Word, where He reveals Himself to us.

Ellen Banks Elwell

The will of God may lead us on a winding road that doesn't make sense, even to the most mature mind. But when the way gets puzzling, we can still trust in the omniscience of God. He knows the end from the beginning, and we can trust His character, knowing that His plans are aimed at accomplishing the best goals.

Donna Morley

In the small measure in which we have come to put self aside and to wait for God's direction, we have found, and will find, reality in a two-way communication with God.

Edith Schaeffer

God's Word . . . acts as a spiritual sobriety test. The Holy Spirit, the Spirit of truth, gave it to us to enable us to escape walking anymore by the foolish, darkened influence of our own hearts. We must place it above our own feelings and intellect and submit to its judgment. While ignorant, self-flattering people prefer their own subjective brand of guidance, we can trust God's Word to tell us the truth and nothing but the truth, so help us, God. Commit yourself right now to allowing the truth of God's Word to impact your life even when it makes you feel uncomfortable.

Cheryl V. Ford

How exciting it is to know that God stands ever ready to reveal His will to us by His Spirit through His Word.

Tom Elliff

The Bible is our source of direction regarding God's moral will. It outlines for us a clear route to follow.

Sheila Cragg

God is not a God afar off. He is close at hand, and the Bible surely teaches that Christians have an obligation to ask the Lord's will in their walk. In most of their walk they will find that the principles set down in the Scriptures are adequate.

Francis A. Schaeffer

Jesus once compared Himself to a shepherd and His people to a flock of sheep. He said a good shepherd "calls his own sheep by name and leads them out . . . his sheep follow him because they know his voice" (John 10:3-4). . . .

Do you know Jesus? Can you recognize His voice? Is He the love of your life? Jesus is calling you to follow Him. His Spirit is calling you by name. If you hear His voice, you will come to love Him.

Philip Graham Ryken

Perhaps you are at a personal crossroads. Some Christians wonder what God wants them to do with their lives. Others contemplate a change of career, or the pursuit of a new educational opportunity, or the possibility of marriage, or a change of ministry within the church. Still others wrestle with deep spiritual questions, wondering who Jesus Christ is or if the Bible is really true.

The thing to do at such times is to recognize that you are standing at the crossroads. Two roads stretch before you. You can go in only one of two directions. Either you can keep going the way you have been going, or you can go down a different road altogether. Your destiny depends upon which road you take.

Philip Graham Ryken

Inviting discernment to be our constant friend will remove the uncertainty, worry, and fear that often come when we're standing at the crossroads of a decision. Considering the many decisions we struggle with daily, discernment is essential. It can do much to help make our lives less complicated . . . and more fulfilling. Wouldn't you like that to be true of your life?

Donna Morley

Proverbs 16:33 says, "The lot is cast into the lap, but its every decision is from the Lord." The lot was a method of determining God's will in the Old Testament. I paraphrase that verse this way: "Life is like a roll of the dice, but God is in charge of how the numbers come up." Because that is true, you can trust Him to give you whatever wisdom you need to make wise decisions and to bring about proper outcomes so that you can do His will every day of your life.

What's the most important factor? Guideability! "Delight yourself in the Lord and he will give you the desires of your heart" (Psalm 37:4). As you delight yourself in the Lord, His desires are going to become your desires. You are going to be changed on the inside so that the things you really want are the things God wants for you.

Can you discover God's will for your life? Thank God, the answer is yes! How do you discover God's will? You discover God's will today the same way the people of God have always discovered His will: step by step by step.

God has promised to guide you safely on your journey through this life. You can depend on that. He has said He will be your guide even to the end. He has promised, and He cannot fail. Therefore . . . if you are truly willing to do God's will, you will do it!

Ray Pritchard

Do you know that in a race all the runners run, but only one gets the prize? Run in such a way as to get the prize. Everyone who competes in the games goes into strict training. They do it to get a crown that will not last; but we do it to get a crown that will last forever.

1 CORINTHIANS 9:24-25

beyond

Running the Race

today

LOVE AND SERVE

CHRIST IN SUCH A

WAY THAT YOU WIN

THE RACE AND RECEIVE

HIS APPROVAL.

Tony Evans

In these days of the twenty-first century, you have more information than ever before on how to keep your body fit—through physical training and careful nourishment. But where can you find wisdom for becoming spiritually fit—through strengthening and nourishing your faith?

The apostle Paul compared the Christian life to a race in which the spiritually fit believer earns a crown. Run in such a way as to get that prize.

With heaven in our hearts, we must stay focused and alert, pressing toward the upward call, running to win our race.

Cheryl V. Ford

Life is a distance marathon; it's not a one-mile race.

Sheila Cragg

"Small is the gate and narrow the road that leads to life," taught Jesus, "and only a few find it" (Matthew 7:14). What makes the road so narrow is the fact that only one person, the Lord, knows where it is, and therefore it is a road that cannot be found or traveled apart from vital relationship with Him.

Mike Mason

Like superior athletes who spend years training for just one Olympic race, exceptional Christians have to submit to spiritual training. There are no shortcuts.

Richard L. Ganz

Your word is a lamp to my feet and a light for my path.

Psalm 119:105

Train yourself to be godly. For physical training is of some value, but godliness has value for all things, holding promise for both the present life and the life to come.

1 T i m o t h y 4 : 7 - 8

Discipline is the key to becoming proficient at anything, whether it be painting, music, writing, calculus, basketball, golf, chess, or the most sublime art—fly fishing. Discipline is what separates the achievers from the also-rans. And this is doubly true in spiritual matters, because man's sinful nature naturally gravitates to foot-dragging in things spiritual. This is why the apostle Paul unabashedly admonished his young disciple, Timothy, to "train yourself to be godly" (1 Timothy 4:7). The very word *train* has the smell of a good workout. . . . Spiritual sweat is a major component to leading a godly life. No man or woman has ever become godly without it.

R. K e n t H u g h e s

It is godly character that will persevere and finish well regardless of the position or obstacles.

S u s a n H u n t

We are told to "run with patience the race that is set before us." I like the word *run* because it indicates what faith is. Faith is active, not static. It is more than mere belief. Faith is belief with legs on it. The athlete learns to run by running. Reading books about running is not enough. Lectures on running will not suffice. The athlete must get out on the track and begin to learn. Use the faith you have, and it will become stronger faith.

Adrian Rogers

It's been said that an optimist sees a glass half full, while a pessimist sees it half empty. An optimist sees opportunities; a pessimist sees obstacles. . . . We've experienced God's saving power and have seen Him answer prayer, and yet there are times when we let pessimism rob us of the joy of seeing Him work through obstacles in our lives. Don't let that happen to you. Keep your eyes on Christ and trust in His sufficiency. He will never fail you!

John MacArthur

It is the LORD your God you must follow, and him you must revere. Keep his commands and obey him; serve him and hold fast to him.

Deuteronomy 13:4

*S*ometime in the early summer before entering the seventh grade, I wandered over from the baseball field and picked up a tennis racket for the first time . . . and I was hooked!

That fall I determined to become a tennis player. I spent my hoarded savings on one of those old beautifully laminated Davis Imperial tennis rackets—a treasure that I actually took to bed with me. I was disciplined! I played every day after school (except during basketball season) and every weekend. When spring came, I biked to the courts where the local high school team practiced and longingly watched until they finally gave in and let me play with them. The next two summers I took lessons, played some tournaments, and practiced about six to eight hours a day—coming home only when they turned off the lights.

And I became good. Good enough, in fact, that as a twelve-and-a-half-year-old, one-hundred-and-ten-pound freshman, I was second man on the varsity tennis team of my large 3,000-student California high school.

Not only did I play at a high level, I learned that personal discipline is the indispensable key for accomplishing anything in this life. . . .

We will never get anywhere in life without discipline, be it in the arts, business, athletics, or academics. This is doubly so in spiritual matters. In other areas we may be able to claim some innate advantage. An athlete may be born with a strong body, a musician with perfect pitch, or an artist with an eye for perspective. But none of us can claim an innate spiritual advantage. In reality, we are all equally disadvantaged. None of us naturally seeks after God, none is inherently righteous, none instinctively does good (Romans 3:9-18). Therefore, as children of grace, our spiritual discipline is everything—everything! . . .

Do we have the sweat in us? Will we enter the gymnasium of divine discipline? Will we strip away the things that hold us back? Will we discipline ourselves through the power of the Holy Spirit?

I invite you to some sanctifying sweat—to some pain and great gain.

R. KENT HUGHES

We're not competing against anyone else. God has set the right course for us. Some Christians will run the spiritual race a lot faster than we will and others a lot slower. Cheer on those who pass us by and lovingly encourage those who lag behind.

Sheila Cragg

If you are not dead yet, you are not finished yet. You still have time to get in the race! . . . You may have stumbled coming out of the blocks. You may have tripped up during the race. You may even be starting the race a little late, but God can help you make up for lost time. He can help you pick up speed in the last half of the race and cover more ground in less time than the average runner. . . .

[God] loves to dispense His grace. If you will come to God with your regrets and your failures, and start loving and serving Him as the driving force in your life, He has an unmistakable, amazing way of using even failure to bring about success.

There is only one passion in life worth your total pursuit. And that is to love and serve Christ in such a way that you win the race and receive His approval.

Tony Evans

[Scripture] pictures the Christian life as a war, a race, and a fight. We depend on God's energy, power, and strength, but we are by no means passive. We're commanded to apply ourselves to good deeds, resist the devil, bring our bodies under subjection, walk in wisdom, press toward the prize, cleanse ourselves from all filthiness of flesh and spirit, work out our salvation with fear and trembling, and perfect holiness in the fear of God. Those are calls to fervent action.

In Ephesians 6:10-11 (NASB) Paul says, "Be strong in the . . . strength of His might. Put on the full armor of God." That's the balance. God supplies the resources; we supply the effort.

John MacArthur

The eternal exchange of our doubt for His faith leads to a daily trust in the Lord Jesus Christ "till glory shines." He triumphed by faith, and He expects us to do the same as we count on Him to develop in us and to display through us a similar faith along life's way.

Stephen F. Olford

I run in the path of your commands, for you have set my heart free.

Psalm 119:32

Two great passions [energize] my life. The one is a passion for God. James 4:8 has marked me: "Draw near to God, and he will draw near to you" [paraphrased]. To commune with God by faith in deep personal fellowship is the highest fulfillment one can experience. I have tasted and seen that the Lord is good, and I want more.

My other passion is for Holy Scripture, the primary vehicle for bringing us near to God. It is perhaps expected that a seminary teacher will show a certain reserve or formality with the Bible, to maintain his professional bearing. But I can't do that. I love the Bible. "The words that I speak to you, they are spirit and they are life," Jesus said in John 6:63 [paraphrased]. Spirit and life! What else is there worth having? And how else are they to be found, but through the Word of God?

Raymond C. Ortlund, Jr.

Staying on track in life means going down the biblical path. The psalmist loved, read, meditated on, and prayed through God's Word. As he did those things, he discovered that the Bible is like a smooth pathway for a difficult journey. . . . The ancient path, the good way, is the Bible.

Philip Graham Ryken

Walking with the Lord isn't intended to be constantly wearying or unbearably burdensome. Even on difficult days, we can know and experience the truth of what it means to be surrounded by God's grace, forgiveness, and love.

Debra Evans

We should not be surprised when living obediently is difficult. Neither should we be surprised to find ourselves often face to face with temptation. If we desire to do what is right, how do we handle these frequent confrontations?

Too often we cry out to God for strength even as we run headlong after sin. We ask God to stop us from disobedience as we are in pursuit of it, and then we wonder why He failed us. We lead ourselves into temptation and then whine that God does nothing to get us out. . . .

Strength comes not in our resistance but in our obedience. To put it very simply, we avoid disobedience by obedience. When we are doing what is right, we are avoiding what is wrong. Fill your life with righteousness to make less room for unrighteousness. It is when we turn from sin that the Holy Spirit gives us strength not to sin.

David Haney

Do you desire a more solid, robust faith? Faith grows greater by the continual exercise of it; therefore, you should intentionally exercise it daily. If you make this your practice, then, soon to God's glory, your enemies will fall before you, whether by threes or by thousands. As C. H. Spurgeon said, "Little faith will bring your souls to heaven, but great faith will bring heaven to your souls."

Cheryl V. Ford

"Ask," Jesus promised, "and it will be given to you." Why? Because the profoundest desires, wishes, dreams, and hopes of a child of God turn out to be the very stuff of the Lord's own will. If He promises to "give you the desires of your heart" (Psalm 37:4), it is because He is the one who has planted those desires in the first place.

Mike Mason

Fight the good fight of the faith. Take hold of the eternal life to which you were called when you made your good confession in the presence of many witnesses.

1 Timothy 6:12

hatever you do, work at it with all your heart, as working for the Lord, not for men, since you know that you will receive an inheritance from the Lord as a reward. It is the Lord Christ you are serving.

COLOSSIANS 3:23-24

beyond
today

Nine to Five

WE WORK FOR THE LORD....

HE PROMISES A REWARD

FOR WORK WELL DONE

FOR HIM. IN REALITY,

OUR WORK IS NEVER

THANKLESS IF WE'RE

CHILDREN OF THE KING.

Lael F. Arrington

Work matters—of course it does! Whether or not we've established ourselves in a career, the numerous tasks of maintaining our lives create hours of work every day.

Your work matters to God—so much that He wants to hold the place of "Ultimate Employer." Go to work for Him and realize true job satisfaction. ❧

The most precious thing a human being has to give is time. There is so very little of it, after all, in a life. Minutes in an hour, hours in a day, days in a week, weeks in a year, years in a life. It all goes so swiftly! And what has been done with it?

Edith Schaeffer

Respect those who work hard among you, who are over you in the Lord and who admonish you. Hold them in the highest regard in love because of their work. Live in peace with each other. And we urge you, brothers, warn those who are idle, encourage the timid, help the weak, be patient with everyone.

1 Thessalonians 5:12-14

If we're going to model and teach a biblical work ethic to our children, we need to see our work and our role as God sees them.

When we look at ourselves in the mirror of God's Word, we see a [person] made for work. Our children should also understand that they were made for work as well.

Lael F. Arrington

The LORD God took the man and put him in the Garden of Eden to work it and take care of it.

Genesis 2:15

Therefore, my dear brothers, stand firm. Let nothing move you. Always give yourselves fully to the work of the Lord, because you know that your labor in the Lord is not in vain.

1 Corinthians 15:58

I thank Christ Jesus our Lord, who has given me strength, that he considered me faithful, appointing me to his service.

1 Timothy 1:12

One of Wellington's officers, when commanded to go on some perilous duty, lingered a moment as if afraid, and then said, "Let me have one clasp of your all-conquering hand before I go; and then I can do it." Seek the clasp of Christ's hand before every bit of work, every hard task, every battle, every good deed. Bend your head in the dewy freshness of every morning, ere you go forth to meet the day's duties and perils, and wait for the benediction of Christ, as He lays His hands upon you. They are hands of blessing. Their touch will inspire you for courage and strength and all beautiful and noble living.

J. R. Miller

Whatever your hand finds to do, do it with all your might.

Ecclesiastes 9:10

Genuine Christians recognize that holiness is necessary for effective service to God. Holiness and usefulness are linked together.

Sheila Cragg

God is not unjust; he will not forget your work and the love you have shown him as you have helped his people and continue to help them. . . . We do not want you to become lazy, but to imitate those who through faith and patience inherit what has been promised.

Hebrews 6:10, 12

More than ever, I believe the Bible is true, that it can be applied to all of life as it is actually lived, moment by moment, before the wondrous reality of Christ's love. No matter where we have been, we can walk with Jesus in newness of life, set free from the strongholds of the past and supernaturally strengthened by the Holy Spirit for the work "God prepared in advance for us to do" (Ephesians 2:10).

Debra Evans

"As long as it is day, we must do the work of him who sent me. Night is coming, when no one can work."

John 9:4

Since there is no room for sloth or indolence in the Lord's work, Paul exhorts us not to lag behind in diligence (Romans 12:11 NASB). Solomon counsels us, "Whatever your hand finds to do, verily, do it will all your might; for there is no activity or planning or wisdom in Sheol [the grave]" (Ecclesiastes 9:10 NASB). We need to make the most of whatever time the Lord has given us on earth. Many opportunities for Christian service come our way only once, and we must take advantage of them.

John MacArthur

Even the so-called secular areas of life are to be sanctified, so that Jesus will be glorified in everything. Because He now lives in me, every day is a holy day, every time is a sacred time, and every task is a sacred task. The spiritual life is seven days a week. What does it mean to do everything "in the name of the Lord Jesus"? . . . to do everything in the name of Jesus means to do only that which He could endorse or approve. All that we do should be consistent with His character. We ought to do or say nothing that we could not sign Jesus' name to!

Adrian Rogers

Ask what thy work in the world is—that for which thou wast born, to which thou wast appointed, on account of which thou wast conceived in the creative thought of God. That there is a divine purpose in thy being is indubitable. Seek that thou mayest be permitted to realize it. And never doubt that thou hast been endowed with all the special aptitudes which that purpose may demand. God has formed thee for it, storing thy mind with all that He knew to be requisite for thy life work. It is thy part to elaborate and improve to the utmost the . . . talents which thou hast.

F. B. Meyer

Paul described the Philippians as a people "whose God is their belly" (3:19 KJV). . . . There are people who think of nothing but how they are going to sauté some culinary delight, sauce it, and present it to their palates with the proper vintage. . . . Christians ought to be free to enjoy life's pleasures. Good food, recreation, and diversions are important parts of life—in proper perspective. We all know that "All work and no play makes Jack a dull boy." But we must remember, too, that all play and no work makes Jack an idolater!

R. Kent Hughes

*O*ur children are absorbing a utilitarian work ethic: work is a means to an end, namely, leisure time and money to spend. . . . Work is a necessary evil endured from coffee break to lunchtime to afternoon break to quitting time, so that we can afford to enjoy ourselves in the leisure time that makes life worth living. This can be a battle of perspective for both our children and ourselves. . . .

How do we renew our minds to resist the relentless calls to acquire more toys and endure the weekday work-grind so we can play with them on the weekend? . . .

God's Word doesn't just warn us about greed; it calls us to a view of service, and by extension our work, that sees whatever we do as ministry and an opportunity to use our God-given gifts and talents. . . .

God's offer of abundant life, indifferent to the pursuit of abundant possessions, is so much richer. C. S. Lewis provides a stunning analogy. In his sermon "The Weight of Glory," he chides us: "Our Lord finds our desires not too strong, but too weak. We are half-hearted creatures fooling about with drink and sex and [greedy] ambition when infinite joy is offered us, like an ignorant child who wants to go on making mud pies in a slum because he cannot imagine what is meant by the offer of a holiday at the beach."

The fun, the ambition that drives our children into a lifetime of work and service should not be the sparkle of new "toys," but the development of their unique gifting before God.

LAEL F. ARRINGTON

We often separate the secular from the sacred. Our regular work is not considered a service to the Lord. . . . When we're seeking and obeying His guidance, every mundane duty, every great or small task, everything we do at any given moment can become sacred acts of grace.

Sheila Cragg

Daniel was a very busy man. He was Grand Vizier of the Babylonian empire and had many and very important duties to perform. Jealous men were watching to detect the slightest mistake in his administration. But he found time to go aside three times every day for prayer and thanksgiving. Daniel was a most efficient official. His enemies were unable to charge him with any error or fault. Prayer through which men obtain wisdom and power from on high helps make men efficient. Busy men in responsible positions cannot afford to neglect prayer. Persecution did not turn Daniel aside from his prayer habit. Though it exposed him to the sentence of death, he prayed and gave thanks as usual. Shame on us that we too often allow trifles to keep us from prayer.

Charles A. Cook

Set this on your hearts: Your work matters to God! . . . We meet God the Creator as a worker in Genesis 1:1—2:2. In fact, that entire section is a log of God's work, ending with the statement that upon completion "[He] rested from all the work of creating that he had done." . . . God's being a worker endows all legitimate work with an intrinsic dignity.

Inherent within the human personality is a God-given creativity, but carried to excess, we become workaholics and subject to occupational neuroses and burnout. The cares of this world, which God never intended us to carry, press in upon us until we can hardly breathe. This is not restricted to busy executives; it can be right at the heart of ministry. It is possible for God's servants to be intensely overworked doing the Lord's work. We need to "beware the barrenness of a busy life!" Or as a great Bible teacher in Britain put it, "Beware lest service sap spirituality." The danger is that Christian service can become religious activism until, ultimately, it smothers us. Therefore, let us maintain a Christian alertness.

Stephen F. Olford

Life is not segmented into sacred and secular. All of life is sacred because it is lived in His presence.

Susan Hunt

For we are God's workmanship, created in Christ Jesus to do good
works, which God prepared in advance for us to do.

Ephesians 2:10

There are certain things that are given as absolutely sinful in the
Scripture, and these things we as Christians should not do. . . . But
then *everything else is spiritual.* The painting of a picture, the work
of a good shoemaker, the doctor, the lawyer—all these things are
spiritual if they are done within the circle of what is taught in
Scripture, looking to the Lord day by day for His help.

Francis A. Schaeffer

Many of us think that because someone in authority gives the plan,
it's the plan we have to follow. But unless that plan agrees with
God's plan, it's the wrong plan. What God wants you to understand is that your ultimate allegiance is not to this world and its
system. It's not to the popular trends in society, and it's not to what
everyone else wants for your life. The issue for you as a Christian
is, what does God want?

Tony Evans

Work is our God-given responsibility. Remember Genesis 2:15? Adam was put in the garden "to work it," and this was before the Fall. Then in verse 18 God purposed to make Eve to be Adam's "suitable helper" so he would not be alone. This meant that Eve was to help Adam work and tend the garden. Man and woman were created primarily for relationship and work, not leisure. And the work included both manual labor (caring for the garden) and intellectual labor (some aspects of caring for the garden, naming the animals).

Lael F. Arrington

As God's masterworks, we have been "created in Christ Jesus to do good works, which God prepared in advance for us to do." Each of us has an eternally designed work assignment that includes the task, the ability, and a place to serve. Whatever the task to which He has called you, you will be equipped for it as surely as a bird is made for flight. And in doing the works He has called you to do, you will be both more and more His workmanship and more and more your true self.

The practical implications of this are stupendous. There is no secular/sacred distinction, for all honest work done for the Lord is sacred. . . . There are no first-class and second-class Christians

because of their varying jobs. All work is sacramental in nature, be it checking groceries, selling futures, cleaning teeth, driving a street sweeper, teaching, or painting trim. Everything we do ought to be done to the glory of God.

R. Kent Hughes

Just as the slave must "will" the will of his master, our usefulness to Jesus depends on the extent to which we will the will of God. We are not robots. Rather, in love we choose to return to the position of obedient dependence on God in which He created us. This may seem an unpleasant idea to some, but as God's creatures this "slaveness" is the only place of joy and the only place of usefulness.

Francis A. Schaeffer

All Scripture is God-breathed and is useful for teaching, rebuking, correcting and training in righteousness, so that the man of God may be thoroughly equipped for every good work.

2 Timothy 3:16-17

God is able to make all grace abound to you, so that in all things at all times, having all that you need, you will abound in every good work.

2 Corinthians 9:8

When we look at the example of work that God set for man, we find a ratio of six days of work to one day of leisure (Exodus 20:9-11). This is an interesting balance. . . . God knew that we have more to gain from work than from leisure. . . .

Check out Ecclesiastes 5:18-19. . . . Solomon, the wisest man on earth, recognized that it's "good and proper . . . to find satisfaction in our toilsome labor" and that being "happy in our work . . . is a gift of God." We are created to work and to find happiness and fulfillment in work.

Lael F. Arrington

Work challenges us—makes us grow in character, skill, and creativity. Learning to take responsibility for hard work, day-in and day-out over the long haul, develops perseverance, one of the major traits God wants to build into our lives.

Lael F. Arrington

It is natural—actually quite easy—to be enthusiastic if your work is prominent, but less natural the more hidden it is, as the conductor of a great symphony orchestra once revealed when asked which was the most difficult instrument to play. "Second fiddle," he answered.

"We can get plenty of first violinists. But to get someone who will play second violin with enthusiasm—that is a problem!"

And so it is. But actually, doing one's work with enthusiasm, even if hidden, plays for an audience far greater than that of the most famous symphony orchestras or world champion sports teams! If we could but really see this, our enthusiasm would never flag. . . .

"Whatever you do," Paul told the Colossians, "work at it with all your heart, as working for the Lord, not for men" (Colossians 3:23).

R. Kent Hughes

Inherent within the human personality is a God-given creativity, but carried to excess, we become workaholics and subject to occupational neuroses and burnout. The cares of this world, which God never intended us to carry, press in upon us until we can hardly breathe. This is not restricted to busy executives; it can be right at the heart of ministry. It is possible for God's servants to be intensely overworked doing the Lord's work. We need to "beware the barrenness of a busy life!" Or as a great Bible teacher in Britain put it, "Beware lest service sap spirituality." The danger is that Christian service can become religious activism until, ultimately, it smothers us. Therefore, let us maintain a Christian alertness.

Stephen F. Olford

CHAPTER FIVE

I can do everything through him who gives me strength.

PHILIPPIANS 4:13

Power for Life

BEING "PLUGGED INTO" THE

POWER OF GOD THROUGH

THE HOLY SPIRIT IS NOT

SOME SORT OF MYSTICAL

EXPERIENCE RESERVED FOR

THE VERY SPIRITUAL. IT IS

SIMPLY AN AWARENESS OF

MY EMPTINESS WITHOUT

HIM—THAT HE IS MY

STRENGTH, MY SHIELD.

Nancie Carmichael

Because you're human, you know

what it feels like to reach the end of your own resources—physically,

emotionally, and spiritually. But because of His great love and

because He "remembers that we are dust," God provides every-

thing—everything!—we need to live for Him day by day.

Tap into the ultimate power source. ❧

True faith depends not at all upon itself, nor upon its own system of piety, but rather on the Lord alone and His faithfulness.

Mike Mason

The power for godly living is the Holy Spirit, who indwells you. As you yield to Him through prayer and obedience to God's Word, the characteristics of a true saint become increasingly evident in your life.

John MacArthur

To reign, God must have power. And to reign sovereignly, He must have all power. Omnipotent means simply this: all-powerful. God possesses an incomprehensible store of power.

R. Kent Hughes

We can rely on God to be consistent, reliable, and unchangeable. "Jesus Christ is the same yesterday and today and forever" (Hebrews 13:8). God's nature is absolutely unchangeable. God is always the same. . . . God is who He says He is. What He has promised He will perform. He keeps His word.

Sheila Cragg

While there is godly independence, one that keeps us from being influenced by the world (Ephesians 4:14), there is also sinful independence. It keeps us from admitting to ourselves that we need God, making us feel self-sufficient.

Donna Morley

It is God who arms me with strength and makes my way perfect.

2 Samuel 22:33

Nothing can keep you and me from living lives of power, meaning, and vibrancy, from making decisions based on the transcendent, biblical principles that should guide our lives. . . . When we decide to live by them, we are freed up to live with passion and principle, joy and calling.

Richard L. Ganz

Here, then, is a wonderful thing, that if you believe in the Lord Jesus Christ, He becomes your representative. And everything He did, He did for you, so that you have done it in Him.

Martyn Lloyd-Jones

So do not fear, for I am with you; do not be dismayed, for I am your God. I will strengthen you and help you; I will uphold you with my righteous right hand.

Isaiah 41:10

We must make a deliberate choice to respond to God rather than to resist His leadership and suffer serious consequences.

Tom Elliff

We were in the slave market of sin, in such bondage that there was no way of escape. We could not earn our way out. We could never make ourselves worthy of deliverance. But God reached down with unmerited love and saved us, as John so clearly explained: "This is love: not that we loved God, but that he loved us and sent his Son as an atoning sacrifice for our sins" (1 John 4:10).

R. Kent Hughes

Goodness matters. It matters to God who is goodness that is completely pure. His love is unlimited. . . . We must not pretend to be good and sufficient in ourselves as we limp along, but be real and go to the actual source of life.

Susan Schaeffer Macaulay

If anyone serves, he should do it with the strength God provides, so that in all things God may be praised through Jesus Christ.

1 Peter 4:11

There are two factors in salvation: the basis and the instrument. The basis of our salvation is the finished work of Jesus Christ, without a hair's breadth of any human good works added to the scale. The instrument by which we share in this salvation is our faith, our believing God. Our faith does not have saving value. We're not saved on the basis of our faith. We're saved only on the basis of the finished work of Jesus Christ. But the instrument by which we share in this is our faith. Our faith links us to the salvation Christ provides. Our faith is the empty hands that accept the gift of salvation.

Francis A. Schaeffer

Therefore, strengthen your feeble arms and weak knees. "Make level paths for your feet," so that the lame may not be disabled, but rather healed.

Hebrews 12:12-13

Our narcissistic, self-absorbed, self-centered society constantly tells us that we are the kings of our own little worlds, that we have the right to be what we want to be, to set our own goals, pursue our own dreams, choose our own lifestyles, and ignore those who tell us what to do or stand in our way. The two hallmarks of our culture are personal rights and personal freedom. But the Bible in no uncertain terms teaches the very opposite. Scripture reveals God as the rightful owner of all men because He created them and of all of us who are believers because He is our Father who purchased us.

John MacArthur

This is a God-created and God-sustained world. If we do things God's way, He is responsible for the results. If we do not do things His way, we become responsible for the results.

Timothy M. Warner

I pray that out of his glorious riches he may strengthen you with power through his Spirit in your inner being, so that Christ may dwell in your hearts through faith.

Ephesians 3:16-17

*O*f all the truths that I have finally learned, I do not know of one that is more encouraging and life-changing than the marvelous and vital truth that God is alive and well in me through His Son, Jesus Christ.

Yet it is possible to be a Christian and not be aware of this. Paul had to remind the believers at Corinth, "What? know ye not that your body is the temple of the Holy Ghost which is in you, which ye have of God, and ye are not your own?" (1 Corinthians 6:19 KJV). He reminded them again in 2 Corinthians 6:16 (KJV), "ye are the temple of the living God; as God hath said, 'I will dwell in them, and walk in them; and I will be their God, and they shall be my people.'"

It may take us this lifetime and into eternity to finally understand and grasp all that this means, but I know this: God meant it to be a bright, living reality in our daily lives! God wants to change the mundane into the momentous and drudgery into delight. He wants to turn struggle into victory.

ADRIAN ROGERS

We need the continual filling of the Spirit because we are leaky vessels. As each day wears on, as the pressures of life ebb and flow, we may find ourselves depending less on the Holy Spirit and more on our own resources to get ourselves out of trouble or to handle the crises of life. And so we become bossy or petty or unkind or impatient or just plain cranky and hard to live with. . . . That's why we need to come to the Lord many times each day, asking for a new and fresh infilling of the Spirit. We need new power, new blessing, new strength to face the challenges of the day.

Ray Pritchard

"Not by might nor by power, but by my Spirit," says the LORD Almighty.

Zechariah 4:6

God delights in our availability and will empower us. He doesn't need us but chooses to use us for His service. Service is the channel for the power of God, the means by which our naturally selfish lives can be refocused.

Richard L. Ganz

One of the first things we have to learn as Christians is not to trust our own thinking or rely on our own instincts. We now have the mind of Christ (1 Corinthians 2:16), and His is the only mind we can rely on. When we are faithful and obedient to our Lord, we will think like Him, act like Him, love like Him, and in every possible way behave like Him, so that "whether we are awake or asleep, we may live together with him" (1 Thessalonians 5:10).

John MacArthur

What we men call self-reliance or doing it our way or being our own man is really the grace of God letting us have a little rope until we get hung up and discover . . . that God is the One in charge. He's calling all the shots.

Tony Evans

We belong to God. He may do with us as He wishes. There is something deep within us that rebels at being reminded of that elemental truth. But truth it is. Indeed, our rebellion in the face of it is a reminder of how much we still want to be at the center of the universe, with God serving us. That is the heart of all idolatry.

D. A. Carson

As recipients of redemption, we are empowered to reflect our Redeemer. We live in His presence. It is our privilege and responsibility to reflect Him in all of life.

Susan Hunt

A wise man has great power, and a man of knowledge increases strength.

Proverbs 24:5

We need the power of Christ for our lives, whether for justification or for sanctification, and it is only possible to have this power through Jesus Christ, and the agency by which we acquire this power is the indwelling Holy Spirit. . . . If I am going to walk in this present life according to my high calling as a Christian, I need a strength that is higher than my own strength. I need the power of Christ.

Francis A. Schaeffer

Recognize your weaknesses and rely totally on God's resources. Then He will hear your prayers and minister to your needs. That's where happiness begins!

John MacArthur

The peace of God, which transcends all understanding, will guard your hearts and your minds in Christ Jesus.

PHILIPPIANS 4:7

Rest for Your Soul

In your busy life, do you have a quiet time and a quiet place where consistently, day by day, you can spend time in prayer with the Lord?... Quiet places where we spend quiet times will be places and times of intimate communion with God.

Tom Elliff

beyond
today

Life can be relentless with the clamor of technology and media, with on-the-job stresses, with relationship struggles. Where can you go to find an oasis of peace and quiet?

Near to the heart of God.

In Psalm 37:7 the psalmist exhorts, "Rest in the Lord, and wait patiently for Him" (NKJV). In the Hebrew, the word *rest* virtually means "quit nagging," "be silent to the Lord." When we have reached that ultimate communion with the indwelling Lord Jesus Christ, we know how to appropriate divine life, taking from Him all that we need. We need not nag Him. We simply rest in Him and in His gracious purpose for our lives.

S t e p h e n   F .   O l f o r d

The created order is such that humankind needs a rest—in the pattern of a seven-day cycle. . . . God's rhythm is best for men and women because God created them.

R .   K e n t   H u g h e s

He makes me lie down in green pastures, he leads me beside quiet waters, he restores my soul.

P s a l m   2 3 : 2 - 3

You will keep in perfect peace him whose mind is steadfast, because he trusts in you.

I s a i a h   2 6 : 3

Sabbath-keeping means action, not inaction. . . . We do not keep the Sabbath holy by lounging around doing nothing. We are to rest from the business of our earthly calling in order to prosecute the business of our heavenly calling. If we do not spend the day doing the latter, we fail to keep it holy.

Sabbath-keeping is not a tedious burden, but a joyful privilege. The Sabbath is not a fast, but a feast, a day for rejoicing in the works of a gracious God, and joy must be its temper throughout.

J. I. Packer

"If you keep your feet from breaking the Sabbath
    and from doing as you please on my holy day,
if you call the Sabbath a delight
    and the LORD'S holy day honorable,
and if you honor it by not going your own way
    and not doing as you please or speaking idle words
then you will find your joy in the LORD,
    and I will cause you to ride on the heights of the land
    and to feast on the inheritance of your father Jacob."
    The mouth of the Lord has spoken.

Isaiah 58:13-14

Seek peace and pursue it.

Psalm 34:14

We are so busy thinking, discussing, defending, inquiring, or preaching and teaching and working, that we have no time, and no leisure of heart for quiet contemplation, without which the exercise of the intellect upon Christ's truth will not feed, and busy activity in Christ's cause may starve the soul.

Alexander MacLaren

Jesus went into the hills to find rest and spiritual refuge. Once when he was weary after ministering to the hungering crowds, He offered this invitation to His disciples: "'Come with me by your-selves to a quiet place and get some rest.' So they went away by themselves in a boat to a solitary place" (Mark 6:31-32).

Sheila Cragg

A balance between work and leisure creates an agreeable atmos-phere in a life or a home, contrasting strongly with the atmosphere created by much rush and stress. One atmosphere tends toward anxiety and dissatisfaction; the other is contented and peaceful.

Susan Schaeffer Macaulay

*J*esus calls us, "Come to me, all you who are weary and burdened, and I will give you rest. Take my yoke upon you and learn from me, for I am gentle and humble in heart, and you will find rest for your souls. For my yoke is easy and my burden is light" (Matthew 11:28-30).

Long ago I learned those verses without thinking of them as a personal invitation to find rest for my soul, to hear God with my heart, to listen to His Word until I found spiritual rest. I often questioned how Jesus' yoke could be easy to carry and His burden light when so much suffering and evil darkened our world. Then I came to realize that sin's heavy yoke overburdens us with guilt and shame, while Christ's light yoke redeems us with forgiveness and grace. God has assured us that "it is for freedom that Christ has set us free. Stand firm, then, and do not let yourselves be burdened again by a yoke of slavery" (Galatians 5:1).

Take off sin's yoke, the one that is rough, hard, and wearisome; put on the sacred yoke, the one that is pure, holy, and restful.

SHEILA CRAGG

Because God is at peace with us, because He has declared us justified, because we have returned to the purpose of our creation, we can in the present have a relationship with God and can have true peace in our heart. People struggle like mad to have peace in their hearts. They try all kinds of psychological methods to find some point of integration. But all such efforts lead only to disappointment unless it involves the relationship and the purpose for which we were created. The only way we can return to that purpose and to that relationship is by having our guilt before God removed on the basis of Christ's finished work. Once we have thus had our guilt removed, there can be a peace in our hearts that is not false, a peace that will never disappoint us.

Francis A. Schaeffer

How many of you know perfect rest? How many know real peace and quiet? Is there not a warfare going on in you? Is there not a strife and a tension, is there not a conflict? We have to say there is— we are all born like that. . . . There is only one thing in the whole world at this moment that can deal with this warfare and tension and strife. It is the cross of our Lord and Savior, Jesus Christ.

Martyn Lloyd-Jones

After God had worked six days in creation, He sat back and rested—not because He was tired, but that He might enjoy His creation. Then God said, "This is such a good thing to do that I'll share it with my creation."

That's why we celebrate the Lord's Day every Sunday. It is a day set aside for us to enjoy God in the context of worship and to enjoy His created order.

Besides providing a day of rest and worship, God honors His children in other ways. Read Ecclesiastes 5:18, and you'll see that God's reward for you as His child is that you might enjoy His goodness. He says, "I want you to enjoy your labor and its fruit."

So you ought to do things well. Work hard and play hard. If you love your job, you should love the fruit of your job. Solomon says that God has given all of this to us to enjoy.

My point is that if you are honoring God with your money, when He gives you a little extra, and you want to do something fun with it in a way that does not dishonor Him, God says He has given you that extra to enjoy. You don't need to feel guilty for enjoying it either. God is not a miserly giver. Determine you'll be faithful in your stewardship, thank Him for His provisions, and enjoy Him!

Tony Evans

The Sabbath's purpose was to grace God's people—to grace their bodies with the rest of the Genesis rhythm—to grace their souls with heaven's rhythm, providing Israel with respite from their labors so they could focus on God and gratefully commemorate their gracious liberation.

R. Kent Hughes

Jesus needed to balance the busy "people-days" by going to a quiet place to pray, to be alone with His Father. When we are suffering from too much work or the hubbub of lots of people in our days, it is so sweet to withdraw in peace and quietness. For those of us who know Jesus, this can be our most recreational place. There we find ourselves in green pastures with sweet water to drink.

Susan Schaeffer Macaulay

When God's voice rolled down the slopes of Mt. Sinai, the command was most explicit as to its requirements: "Remember the Sabbath day by keeping it holy. Six days you shall labor and do all your work, but the seventh day is a Sabbath to the LORD your God. On it you shall not do any work . . ." (Exodus 20:8-10).

R. Kent Hughes

Jesus spent His free times pursuing relationships—with God, with believers, and with unbelievers. The irony of our fixation on media is that it tends to reduce our face time with other people. The vast majority of what we see on the screen leads away from relationship. Great breadth, little depth. More times to "throw away" or subtly "tear down."

Lael F. Arrington

The longer I live, the more convinced I become that the greatest work of God takes place in the private arena—the quiet place, the quiet time. There God waits for us in order to have sweet communion, resolve anguishing conflict, and bring about a remarkable conformity to His Son, our Lord Jesus Christ.

Tom Elliff

The fruit of righteousness will be peace; the effect of righteousness will be quietness and confidence forever.

Isaiah 32:17

Right thinking brings the peace of God. Right thinking combined with right actions brings the God of peace.

Richard L. Ganz

In repentance and rest is your salvation, in quietness and trust is your strength.

Isaiah 30:15

O infinite God, You conceal within Yourself the final explanation of life's mysteries. For this I trust You. You execute Your will in my life without my help. For this I rest in You. You sanctify all events with divine meaning and purpose, so that I am always safe, no matter what evil befalls me. For this I rejoice in You. With You there, O God, being who You are, everything ultimately will be all right, because all things are moving toward Your glory. O God and Father, be glorified here on the platform of my little life, for Your glory is my eternal security and everlasting joy. In the holy name of Christ, amen.

Raymond C. Ortlund, Jr.

"Peace I leave with you; my peace I give you. I do not give to you as the world gives. Do not let your hearts be troubled and do not be afraid."

John 14:27

The Sabbath was serious because it was the day when you were supposed to focus not on your work, but on giving thanks to God for the work He allowed you to do. It was a time to enjoy the God of work rather than the work itself.

The Sabbath also meant you were trusting God for next week's work. This is powerful, because it means that when you are working in the will of God, you can trust Him for next week's opportunity, next week's promotion, next week's challenges. So instead of knocking yourself out, you say, "God, this is it. I'm done. I'm going to stop working and trust You." . . .

One way to avoid letting work dominate us is to put limitations on it. We are not to be driven by greed. And we are not to work seven days a week so that our spiritual life dries up and dies.

My brother, if you're working so hard that you never get time with God or time with your loved ones, you're working too hard. Your work was never meant to replace God in your life. Work had its limits even with the One who created it. He rested on the seventh day. In imitation, His people are to rest on the Lord's Day.

Tony Evans

My soul finds rest in God alone; my salvation comes from him. . . . Find rest, O my soul, in God alone; my hope comes from him.

Psalm 62:1, 5

Our Lord knows that we'll never feel fully at rest during our earthly journey. He knows that most of what we do daily to maintain our lives and much of what we do for pleasure leaves us tired. He knows that to escape our pain and those empty, lonely moments, we overload them with meaningless activities and anxious thoughts that fatigue us. . . .

The Lord Himself is inviting us to follow Him to a place of peaceful quietness for personal restoration, to find a place of solitude for spiritual recuperation. Come, sit at the place He's set for you. He longs to serve you, so let His healing Word quench your thirst; let His tender mercy refresh your starved soul; let His gracious love awaken your spiritual passion.

Sheila Cragg

If you live a high-demand, stressful life, try to see that the basics stay in place. And none of us should ever forget the place where we are remade—our source of life, the Lord. He promises a life-giving sap for each one. . . . It would be folly not to be sure of this essential time in the daily schedule. We find it in a quiet place and moment, with God's Word and our full attention.

Susan Schaeffer Macaulay

CHAPTER SEVEN

*L*ike newborn babies, crave pure

spiritual milk, so that by it you may

grow up in your salvation, now that

you have tasted that the Lord is good.

1 PETER 2:2-3

Growing in Godliness

WHEN BELIEVERS WANT
TO FIND AND KNOW THE
TRUTH THE WAY SOME
PEOPLE LOOK FOR
NATURAL TREASURES,
WHEN BELIEVERS
CRAVE THE WORD AS
PASSIONATELY AS AN
INFANT CRAVES MILK,
THEY WILL GROW AND
MATURE AND BECOME
LIKE JESUS CHRIST.

John MacArthur

"I don't wanna grow up!"

say the singers on a toy store's commercial. Sometimes you may feel

the same way—it can seem safer to stick with what you know, where

you're at.

But God calls His people to maturity—to grow in godliness,

accepting grown-up responsibilities and grown-up joys. ✣

Holiness and the accountability of surrender to God seem so remote from the realities of daily living. We may desire to be holy, and yet we run from convictions that call us to make godly choices. We flee because of our pride and our tremendous fear of the requirements of holiness.

We need to realize that becoming a godly person is a process and that we will never become completely holy in our lifetime. We all need a beginning place where we can grow in godliness. So pack away the guilt and "shoulds" and feelings of inferiority and unworthiness. Start where you are, and begin this journey with an open heart and willing spirit to become the person the Lord desires you to be.

Sheila Cragg

[Jesus Christ] desires to rule every inch of your heart. When you live your life in submission to His rule, He is able to change you into an extraordinary man or woman.

Richard L. Ganz

Godliness has value for all things, holding promise for both the present life and the life to come.

1 Timothy 4:8

Life by its very definition is a growth process. That which is alive is growing. For example, seedlings grow to be trees, in some cases to heights of several hundred feet. Even when they reach their full height, they exhibit regular growth through the production of new leaves, branches, or fruit.

The principle of growth also holds true in the spiritual realm. An essential, inherent characteristic for everyone in the body of Christ is individual spiritual growth.

John MacArthur

Follow the way of love and eagerly desire spiritual gifts.

1 Corinthians 14:1

Then we will no longer be infants, tossed back and forth by the waves, and blown here and there by every wind of teaching and by the cunning and craftiness of men in their deceitful scheming. Instead, speaking the truth in love, we will in all things grow up into him who is the Head, that is, Christ.

Ephesians 4:14-15

And we, who with unveiled faces all reflect the Lord's glory, are being transformed into his likeness with ever-increasing glory, which comes from the Lord, who is the Spirit.

2 Corinthians 3:18

But grow in the grace and knowledge of our Lord and Savior Jesus Christ.

2 Peter 3:18

We do not have to do with an imaginary Jesus. He is actually there! Christians through the ages have found out that the Rock is *real*, a firm foothold. The Bible is bursting with promises and practical instruction.

Susan Schaeffer Macaulay

The veritable reality is that "All Scripture is God-breathed and is useful for teaching, rebuking, correcting and training in righteousness, so that the man [and woman] of God may be thoroughly equipped for every good work" (2 Timothy 3:16-17). We will only be authentic Masterpieces when we line up with God's truth.

Susan Hunt

Our faith must come to the level of maturity that accepts that God holds us accountable for all our decisions. Sufficient knowledge of His will is always available so that we can respond appropriately.

Tom Elliff

Sow an act, and you reap a habit.

Sow a habit, and you reap a character.

Sow a character, and you reap a destiny for yourself

your family

your church

your world.

The Oxford Dictionary of Quotations

Can you recall a time when you didn't have a sharp ear for godly advice? During such times it's easy to make choices we regret later. . . . When I am proud and overconfident, I feel I do not need to seek wisdom from anyone. Sometimes pride makes me hide the fact that I do not "have it all together." If I let on that I need to grow in wisdom, I reveal that I am not already a super-Christian.

I am learning that I must swallow my pride so that I can be teachable and attentive to wisdom, which is found so abundantly throughout Scripture.

Donna Morley

I pray that you may be active in sharing your faith, so that you will have a full understanding of every good thing we have in Christ.

Philemon 6

Our attitudes and thoughts will grow and change in healthy ways only as we saturate our minds with the truth of God's Word and pray for that truth to be worked out in our lives.

Ellen Banks Elwell

Jesus tells us that "anyone who will not receive the kingdom of God like a little child will never enter it" (Luke 18:17). Ironically, in the family of God to become a little child is to have attained maturity. Spiritual growth means growth in childlikeness. To grow up is to grow down.

Mike Mason

The Christian is a man who does not only believe in the cross; he glories in it!

Martyn Lloyd-Jones

*O*nce you become committed to Christ and start reflecting a Christian character, God prunes your branches in hopes of producing more fruit.

Pruning is the process of trimming off unwanted shoots that can rob the branches of the nourishment they would otherwise receive from the vine. In grape growing, these are called "sucker shoots," little branches that grow where the vine and branch intersect. As they grow larger, they begin to do exactly what their name suggests; they suck away the life-giving sap on its way from the vine to the branch.

Even committed Christians need pruning, and it hurts. When God starts trimming off the stuff that should not be in our lives, it's painful. Now God knows that, but like a good father, He weighs the long-term benefit against the short-term discomfort and does what needs to be done.

TONY EVANS

You may be wondering why so many Christians aren't rejoicing in the wonder of an indwelling Christ. They are afraid to make Jesus absolute Lord. They hesitate to throw open every door of the house in which they dwell. Yes, He can come through the front door and go into the living room. He can go into the dining room and kitchen, but there are other rooms of the house they don't want Him to enter. So they keep those doors locked—the doors to those last inner recesses of the human personality. They don't want Him to be at home in their hearts. This is why they need the miraculous operation of the Holy Spirit in their lives.

Stephen E. Olford

We ask God that you may receive from him all wisdom and spiritual understanding for full insight into his will, so that your manner of life may be worthy of the Lord and entirely pleasing to him. We pray that you may bear fruit in active goodness of every kind, and grow in the knowledge of God. May he strengthen you, in his glorious might, with ample power to meet whatever comes with fortitude, patience, and joy; and to give thanks to the Father who has made you fit to share the heritage of God's people in the realm of light.

Colossians 1:9-12 NEB

It is only when I throw myself on His mercy, knowing I cannot—
of my own will—be holy, that I really do begin to comprehend
what it means to be holy.

Nancie Carmichael

The more you and I become conformed to Jesus Christ, the more
we will love righteousness. Our attitudes toward righteousness
and sin will ultimately reveal how closely we are conformed to
Christ. Check out your attitudes and actions. How are you doing?

John MacArthur

Godliness is nurtured not by strain but by reflection: "We all, with
unveiled face beholding as in a mirror the glory of the Lord, are
being transformed into the same image from glory to glory, just as
from the Lord, the Spirit" (2 Corinthians 3:18 NASB). Godly character is the result of a Spirit-empowered life. It is the Spirit who
transforms our character to become more like God's as we continually focus on Him (2 Corinthians 3:18; Galatians 2:12).
Beholding His character and keeping His example continually
before us is the Spirit's way of changing us to be like Him.

Donna Morley

"'Here I am! I stand at the door and knock. If anyone hears my voice and opens the door, I will come in and eat with him, and he with me'" (Revelation 3:20). Jesus is knocking, calling to us, and waiting for us to open the door to a more holy life.

Sheila Cragg

Rejoice in knowing that you belong to God and that He is conforming you to the image of His Son. See every event of this day as part of that process. Yield to the Spirit's prompting, and take heart that God will accomplish His will.

John MacArthur

The Holy Spirit is the most qualified counselor in the universe because He knows us, loves us, encourages us, is patient with us, and prays for us. How thankful we are for His presence in our lives!

Ellen Banks Elwell

The real question is not whether God loves us, but whether He approves of us, whether we are pleasing to Him. One thing is certain: If we are not pleasing to God, He will never be pleasing to us.

Mike Mason

Pursuing holiness is the discipline of confessing and overcoming personal sins, and living in a godly way. Maintaining a godly life means more than laying aside sins; it means taking up godly habits in their place. It means denying self and being crucified with Christ so that we might become more like Him.

Sheila Cragg

John said, "The one who says he abides in [Christ] ought himself to walk in the same manner as He walked" (1 John 2:6 NASB). He added in 2 John 6, "Walk according to His commandments" (NASB). That's how you demonstrate your love for Christ (John 14:15) and please Him in every respect.

As a word of encouragement, a worthy walk is not a walk of sinless perfection. That won't happen until you are fully glorified. But each day you are growing in godliness as a result of the Spirit's transforming work in you (2 Corinthians 3:18). Be faithful to that process. Set your affections on Christ, look to His Word, and rejoice in the privilege of becoming more like Him today.

John MacArthur

Being confident of this, that he who began a good work in you will carry it on to completion until the day of Christ Jesus.

Philippians 1:6

Ask yourself how pleased or how displeased you become if God is praised while you are not, and equally if you are praised while God is not. The mature Christian is content not to have glory given to him, but it troubles him if men are not glorifying God. It pained the dying Puritan Richard Baxter, the outstanding devotional writer of his day, when visitors praised him for his books. "I was but a pen in God's hand," he whispered, "and what praise is due to a pen?" That shows the mentality of the mature; they want to cry every moment, "Give glory to God!—for it is His due, and His alone!"

J. I. Packer

Who is wise and understanding among you? Let him show it by his good life, by deeds done in the humility that comes from wisdom. But if you harbor bitter envy and selfish ambition in your hearts, do not boast about it or deny the truth. Such "wisdom" does not come down from heaven but is earthly, unspiritual, of the devil. For where you have envy and selfish ambition, there you find disorder and every evil practice.

But the wisdom that comes from heaven is first of all pure; then peace-loving, considerate, submissive, full of mercy and good fruit, impartial and sincere. Peacemakers who sow in peace raise a harvest of righteousness.

James 3:13-18

ome near to God and he will

come near to you.

JAMES 4:8

Intimacy with God

beyond today

GOD IS A LIVING GOD, AND HE WANTS TO BE KNOWN. HE MADE MAN IN ORDER THAT MAN MIGHT KNOW HIM AND IN ORDER THAT HE MIGHT HAVE FELLOWSHIP WITH HIM. MAN WAS MEANT TO BE THE COMPANION OF GOD.

Martyn Lloyd-Jones

"To glorify God and enjoy Him forever" is

how the Westminster Catechism describes your purpose on earth.

You—one of the six billion plus people living on earth in this twenty-

first century—are invited to "enjoy" the Creator of the universe! It's an

invitation you can't refuse.

We are spiritual persons; God made us with a need for Him to fill our lives.

Roger C. Palms

For God so loved the world that he gave his one and only Son, that whoever believes in him shall not perish but have eternal life.

John 3:16

As we journey toward holiness, we come to realize our deep longing to know the Lord more personally. Who is this God who has pursued, wooed, and won us? This Lover of our souls—what is He like?

Sheila Cragg

God really is there. He really does exist, and He made us for Himself. Knowing that He is there, and therefore that we do not live in a silent universe, changes everything. To know that we can speak, and there is Someone who will answer fills the vacuum of life that would otherwise be present. And then, when we realize His love for us as individuals—that Christ really did die for us as individuals, for us personally—life is entirely different.

Francis A. Schaeffer

O God, you are my God,

 earnestly I seek you;

my soul thirsts for you,

 my body longs for you. . . .

Because your love is better than life,

 my lips will glorify you.

I will praise you as long as I live,

 and in your name I will lift up my hands.

My soul will be satisfied as with the richest of foods;

 with singing lips my mouth will praise you.

On my bed I remember you;

 I think of you through the watches of the night.

Because you are my help,

 I sing in the shadow of your wings.

Psalm 63:1-7

Loving God is the greatest thing we can do, as Jesus solemnly affirmed: "Love the Lord your God with all your heart and with all your soul and with all your mind. This is the first and greatest commandment" (Matthew 22:37-38).

R . K e n t   H u g h e s

Forget *everything* else. We need to realize the presence of the living God among us. Let everything else be silent. . . . We all need the touch of the power of the living God. And let us continue and wait until we know it.

Martyn Lloyd-Jones

Repentance, faith, prayer, and righteous living all please God because they are expressions of love. That's the overarching principle. Whenever you express your love to Him—whether by words of praise or by acts of obedience—you bring Him joy.

Doesn't it thrill you to know that the God of the universe delights in you? It should! Let that realization motivate you to find as many ways as possible to bring Him joy today.

John MacArthur

Listen to Isaiah: "Seek the LORD while He may be found; call on him while he is near" (Isaiah 55:6). . . . This is the only time for us to respond. Yesterday is past—and with it our opportunity to agree with God. Tomorrow has not arrived—and for any one of us it may never arrive. Only "today" is at our disposal. This is the moment when God wants us to break cycles of hard-hearted indifference and answer His call.

Tom Elliff

Can you remember when you first fell in love with Christ? Can you recall when you were on fire? You were so excited and full of passion. Every time you opened the Word of God, it had something to say to you. Whenever you prayed, all heaven seemed to open up to you! Wherever you went, you had to tell people about Him. Wherever you saw a need, you ministered in the name of Christ. Christ had done so much for you, you had to serve Him!

Can you remember a time like that?

For some of us, such a time was only three months ago. For others, it was three years ago. For others, ten years ago.

The road back to Christ begins by, first, remembering. Memory is the handmaid of revival. Remember the joy that was yours with Him. Can't you recall those times when you first really loved Christ? Get a good look at when you were on fire for Him. Can you remember the pit from which you were dug?

That's where revival begins—remember!

STEVEN J. LAWSON

If you have the courage to let Christ into every room of your life, He will come in and redecorate your life so it is more beautiful than you ever imagined possible. But you'll never know until you start opening those doors.

Ray Pritchard

Revival of the soul and the continual presence of the Lord shall be ours as we, aware of our dependence, humbly offer everything we do as a loving sacrifice to Him.

Donna Morley

We bear His image as a unique spiritual being, designed for intimate relationship with our Savior.

Lael F. Arrington

If you have never entered into a love relationship with God, he is courting you at this moment. He invites you to enter into a love that will never let you go. He calls you to leave behind the sins that carry you here, there, and everywhere in the spiritual desert. He invites you to embrace Jesus Christ.

Philip Graham Ryken

The idea of "practicing the presence of God" puzzled me for a long time, since God is always present with us whether we realize it or not. He may seem distant and even uncaring, though in reality He is always close to us. I finally came to realize that we need to place ourselves in His presence and continually practice seeking Him because our own pain, our own questions, our own unanswered prayers cause us to feel distant from Him.

Sheila Cragg

Love the LORD your God with all your heart and with all your soul and with all your strength.

Deuteronomy 6:5

When we first become Christians we feel that we have finally come to "know" God, and so we have. But as we progress in faith, we go through times when we are less certain that we really know Him at all, and yet we are more certain than ever that He knows us.

Mike Mason

True peace and safety—the place where we really *belong*—is in intimate relationship with Jesus Christ.

Lael F. Arrington

When I was dating Brian [my husband], he used to write me letters all the time. Some told of his care for me; others talked about his desires and goals in life. Letters are important; they expose the heart. What if I ignored his letters, neglecting to read them? Or what if I read them without giving any thought to what he said? Most likely we wouldn't have had much of a relationship. We certainly would not be married today!

Likewise, if I ignored God's letters to me, I wouldn't have much of a relationship with Him either. God wants me to cherish His Word and have a desire to learn every little detail written in it. He wants to tell me so much about Himself.

Donna Morley

There *is* Someone at home in the universe. There is Someone to look up to. There is a light in the darkness. There is a door in the wall. There is *truth* to be found.

Edith Schaeffer

The Spirit himself testifies with our spirit that we are God's children.

Romans 8:16

Be still, and know that I am God.

Psalm 46:10

God desires to share the depths of His heart with you. Are you willing to meet with Him?

Tom Elliff

Blessed are those who have learned to acclaim you, who walk in the light of your presence, O LORD.

Psalm 89:15

Christians have a capacity for spiritual communication with God. So we need to spend adequate time with Him, reading His communication to us and praying in intercession for others and for our own needs.

Edith Schaeffer

If God were as changeable as I am, I would always be seeking a new god on my current terms. But God isn't like me. God doesn't change. We come to Him on His terms; He doesn't come to us on ours. I can meet God, but when I do, I quickly see that God is bigger than my grasp of Him. Listen and understand, Jesus said. It takes

both. People who listen to Jesus and understand what He is saying find what they are searching for. People who listen and understand do at last know who God is, and they know who they are.

Roger C. Palms

The first and most important thing that will help us grow closer to God is a continued and careful living in the Bible. It is not only that we learn facts from the Bible, but it becomes our environment. We are surrounded with a non-Christian environment that continually separates us from God, and this environment draws us away from God. As we read the Bible and live in it daily, it provides the totally opposite atmosphere—namely, the real reality of the existence of God. There is both the seen and unseen world. And as we live in the total moment-by-moment reality of the existence of God and the reality of the unseen world, this will help us grow closer to God.

Francis A. Schaeffer

If you seek God through His Word with an open, receptive heart, you *cannot* miss Him. He will not *let* you miss Him. He will meet you and touch you. He will rekindle your spiritual fire through the power of the Gospel.

Raymond C. Ortlund, Jr.

CHAPTER NINE

Take the helmet of salvation and the sword of the Spirit, which is the word of God. And pray in the Spirit on all occasions with all kinds of prayers and requests.

EPHESIANS 6:17-18

beyond today

Daily Disciplines

IT CAN BE SAID WITH CERTAINTY THAT IF WE MEET THE LORD IN THE SCRIPTURES, WE WILL LONG TO COMMUNE WITH HIM IN PRAYER. AND IF WE MEET THE LORD IN PRAYER, WE WILL LONG TO WALK WITH HIM ALONG BIBLE PATHWAYS. SPENDING TIME WITH GOD IN PRAYER AND IN READING HIS WORD ARE INSEPARABLE TWINS OF SPIRITUAL LIFE.

Tom Elliff

The "secret weapon" for succeeding in the

Christian life is to "keep in step with the Spirit." How can you stay

close to the Lord? Through the twin disciplines of communication with

God and time in His Word. Scripture describes itself as "living" and

"powerful." Have you ever encountered the vitality of God through

His Word? Has it powerfully changed your thinking and plans?

Take up the challenge to study and pray. ❧

Daily Disciplines

A believer who is living a life of practical holiness will know what it is to be completely and continually yielded to God. Such yieldedness implies a once-for-all act of surrender followed by a daily attitude of surrender. This implies a life of development and of discipline.

Stephen F. Olford

All Scripture is God-breathed and is useful for teaching, rebuking, correcting and training in righteousness, so that the man of God may be thoroughly equipped for every good work.

2 Timothy 3:16-17

In John 10:35, Jesus straightforwardly said, "Scripture cannot be broken." Our Lord tells us that not just the ideas of Scripture are true, but the very words with their particular spellings and verb tenses are the source of authority for our lives.

If Jesus takes such a high view of the truth and reliability of Scripture, surely we can, too. Besides, it only makes sense that if God created us and made the rules for living right and joyful lives, He would insure that we received a trustworthy copy of that most important message.

Lael F. Arrington

beyond today

The Christian faith is not true because it works. It works because it is true. No issue is so fundamental both to the searcher and to the believer as the question of truth. The uniqueness and trustworthiness of the Christian faith rest entirely on its claim to be the truth. God, who is the Father of Jesus Christ, is either there or He is not there. Either He has spoken, or He has not spoken. What His revelation claims is either true or false. There are no two ways about it. This stubborn insistence on truth is one thing that lifts the Christian faith out of the common pool of completely personal, relativistic, subjective beliefs. As a young Christian exclaimed to me rather oddly on realizing for the first time the titanic implications of this claim, "I always knew the Christian faith was true, but I never realized it was this true!"

Os Guinness

Jesus said, "Listen to me, believe, and *do what I say*." And "Be not hearers only, but doers also." Duty is doing what is required. This instruction to follow is the price tag of the confident, secure, freely abundant Christian life. No one is ever called to design the pattern of right and wrong. We are asked to fit in. . . . We are asked to choose what is good and to walk in light.

Susan Schaeffer Macaulay

For the word of God is living and active. Sharper than any double-edged sword, it penetrates even to dividing soul and spirit, joints and marrow; it judges the thoughts and attitudes of the heart.

Hebrews 4:12

Just as it takes time to prepare food for a grand banquet, it takes commitment to plan for and feed our spiritual lives. Eating with the Lord at His table is as satisfying as a gourmet feast. But instead of having a magnificent meal, we often settle for airy cotton-candy devotions that leave us empty and dissatisfied. When we don't take enough time with our Lord, we still feel hungry.

Sheila Cragg

The reason that God honors faith is that faith honors Him. Faith is a moral response to the character of God. Therefore, above all things it is faith that gives God pleasure.

Adrian Rogers

Planting the Word in our mind and heart is the discipline of regularly learning and studying the Scripture to help us live according to God's desires, to equip us to serve, and to enable us to share our faith with others.

Sheila Cragg

Pray continually; give thanks in all circumstances, for this is God's will for you in Christ Jesus.

1 Thessalonians 5:17-18

You are an instrument through whom God displays His holiness in the world. If His name is to be hallowed on earth as it is in heaven, it must first be hallowed in your life. That occurs when you believe in Him, understand who He really is, maintain an awareness of His presence, and obey His Word. That high calling sets you apart from every unbeliever (1 Peter 2:9-10). Live today in light of that glorious calling!

John MacArthur

Let the word of Christ dwell in you richly as you teach and admonish one another with all wisdom, and as you sing psalms, hymns and spiritual songs with gratitude in your hearts to God.

Colossians 3:16

Believing in Christ is the key to every victory in the Christian pilgrimage. We cannot merely possess faith; it must possess us. How pervasive is your belief in Christ?

Cheryl V. Ford

Every word of God is flawless; he is a shield to those who take refuge in him.

Proverbs 30:5

It isn't those who say they love God who are true believers, but those who receive Christ and obey His Word. As Jesus said, "If anyone loves Me, he will keep My word (John 14:23 NASB).

John MacArthur

God wants us to bring our everyday needs to Him, even if they appear trivial. He doesn't demand that we approach Him only when we have raised ourselves to some kind of spiritual elevation above the everyday things of life. He comes to meet us where we are, and therein lies His greatness. When we come to Him with our "little things," we do Him great honor.

R. Kent Hughes

His delight is in the law of the LORD, and on his laws he meditates day and night. He is like a tree planted by streams of water, which yields its fruit in season.

Psalm 1:2-3

He that is spiritual is simply the one who has received the Spirit of God. Because of this, he has received life. He has been born from above. He is not merely a natural man who has been improved. Rather than a tadpole who has finally turned into a frog, he is more like a frog who has been transformed into a prince by the kiss of God's grace. Christians are not merely nice characters. They are new creatures.

We must remember, too, that salvation is a matter of receiving Christ through His Spirit into our hearts. It is not merely getting our sins forgiven. Forgiveness is necessary, but it just sets the stage for salvation—the entrance of Christ into our lives. Nor does salvation merely mean going to heaven when we die. That is wonderful, but heaven is the by-product of salvation. Salvation begins with getting the Lord, the life, and the light back into our deadened spirits.

ADRIAN ROGERS

As the rain and the snow come down from heaven, and do not return to it without watering the earth and making it bud and flourish, so that it yields seed for the sower and bread for the eater, so is my word that goes out from my mouth: It will not return to me empty, but will accomplish what I desire and achieve the purpose for which I sent it.

Isaiah 55:11

God is not a vending machine into which I put a quarter and get out a candy bar in purely mechanical fashion. He is personal, and thus in answering prayer He operates on the basis of what He knows is the best and wisest answer to that prayer, and not just in a mechanical reflex.

Francis A. Schaeffer

As true followers of Christ, may we never trade in our spiritual treasures for the things of this world. The sinful nature cries for gratification, and those without true faith have no means by which to resist it. But we who have faith have been given a new nature in Christ. The Holy Spirit gives us the ability to say no to sin. Commit yourself now to refuse to give up any of your spiritual inheritance for worldly advantage.

Cheryl V. Ford

b e y o n d
t o d a y

Man does not live on bread alone but on every word that comes
from the mouth of the LORD.

Deuteronomy 8:3

Make it a point each day to spend time with God. Allow His Word
to instruct and transform your life. While the world builds its values on quicksand, God's Word can be trusted. Despite every
attempt to defeat it, His Word endures because a faithful God
stands behind it.

Cheryl V. Ford

The word of the Lord stands forever.

1 Peter 1:25

Oh, how I love your law!
    I meditate on it all day long.
Your commands make me wiser than my enemies,
    for they are ever with me.
I have more insight than all my teachers,
    for I meditate on your statutes.
I have more understanding than the elders,
    for I obey your precepts.

Psalm 119:97-100

Prayer has been called the "Christian's breath." To neglect it is to neglect God. Only a woman who knows God through prayer can be near to the heart and mind of God.

Donna Morley

Your statutes are wonderful; therefore I obey them. The unfolding of your words gives light; it gives understanding to the simple.

Psalm 119:129-130

The person who doesn't know Christ (even though he may be extremely intelligent and knowledgeable by human standards) cannot understand the wisdom of God. What a huge gift, to know that after we trust Christ, we receive the mind of Christ! Having the mind of Christ doesn't mean that we are perfect or that we think we are God, but rather that we look at life from God's perspective, keeping in mind His truth, His values, and His desires. Through the Word of God, the Holy Spirit helps us think the way Jesus thinks.

Ellen Banks Elwell

All your words are true; all your righteous laws are eternal.

Psalm 119:160

ast all your anxiety on him because

he cares for you.

1   P E T E R   5 : 7

beyond today

Keeping the Faith in Tough Times

EVEN IN THE MIDST

OF THE STORM

HIS PROMISE

IS TRUE: HE

HOLDS US FAST.

Francis A. Schaeffer

They say that "into each life a little rain must fall," but when you're swamped under a deluge, it's natural to wonder why and to call out to the Lord for relief and comfort.

God is near when you are struggling. Trust Him. ❧

God still loves you. He loves you as much in the darkness as He does in the light. Nothing you are going through or ever can go through can separate you from the love of God in Christ Jesus (see Romans 8:35-39). Remember, too, the words of Psalm 34:18, "The LORD is close to the brokenhearted and saves those who are crushed in spirit."

With that thought, let us keep going for the Lord. Be encouraged, child of God. He loves you even in the midst of your pain. He loves you even when you don't love Him. He loves you when you feel utterly alone. He loves you with an everlasting love. Your suffering can take many things away from you—your health, your happiness, your prosperity, your popularity, your friends, your career, even your family. But there's one thing suffering can't take away: it can't take away the love of God.

Ray Pritchard

I'm thankful that God is not like the weather. He is as stable as a rock fortress. I can deal with a difficult situation because I know He won't change. He always listens and is at my side to help me. While others may fail me, He never will. How grateful I am for God's immutable character!

Donna Morley

Disappointments, sorrows, the end of a dream—we all face these. Dead ends, walls we can't seem to climb over. The sharp edges, the pains of life sometimes threaten to overwhelm us. And we cry out, "What is God doing?"

God doesn't have to answer us, of course, but usually He does, either at that moment or later. It is then that we say with overwhelming awe, "Look at what God has done with this that seemed so horrible to me."

In the economy of God, we find that He wastes nothing. From what seems the darkest of nights He often brings the brightest of dawns.

Roger C. Palms

Without God's forgiveness we would have no hope whatsoever. And when we learn to forgive others, a host of life's difficulties suddenly are settled. Forgiveness, we discover, is the starting point for resolving life's most troubling problems.

John MacArthur

Feelings are not the litmus test of truth—it is God's Word against which I can lean, knowing it will hold me.

Nancie Carmichael

Why are we surprised when trying dilemmas knock at our door? We tell God with puzzled voice and furrowed brow, "You must be kidding! I didn't become a believer with this in mind. This is not my idea of the 'abundant life'!" But God knows exactly what He is doing in each of our lives. God assures us that He is powerfully and lovingly at work for our good and His glory in every life situation (Romans 8:28).

Tom Elliff

As you respond differently and excitedly to the challenges that God brings into your life, your entire life experience will change. And not only will your life change, your family and friends will see the vitality and power in your life as you boldly face life's challenges. You will encourage other people, helping them to know that they can face difficulties successfully day by day and step by step.

Richard L. Ganz

Our faith is not just a theoretical thing. It is faith amid temptation. It is faith amid tribulation. It is faith amid the rough-and-tumble of life. What is the rough-and-tumble of your life? . . . Whatever your particular challenges are, your faith in Christ is sufficient to meet them.

Francis A. Schaeffer

*S*ome years ago when airlines first started transatlantic flights to Europe, they noticed that on some flights the plane would arrive an hour or so ahead of schedule without the wear and tear on the engine normally expected for that length of flight.

The airline people couldn't understand it, because they did not know as much about the weather as we do today. So as they began trying to figure out how this could happen, they discovered a weather phenomenon known today as the jet stream.

When an airplane gets into that jet stream, it is propelled forward by the wind so that even though it may be going the same air speed as the plane not in the jet stream, it is really going faster, because it is carried along by the force of the jet stream winds. So rather than fighting the air currents, a plane in the jet stream is actually being carried on the air.

Your trials may have you in turbulence right now. You may feel as if you are flying in the face of a strong wind. . . . What you need to do is catch the "Jesus stream." When you catch that Jesus stream, He will carry you along in the way you need to go.

If you catch the Jesus stream, He will take you where you are trying to go; He will get you there ahead of schedule, and you won't experience all the wear and tear you would if you tried to go it alone. How do you get in the Jesus stream? Just cry out to Him, "Lord, save me!" He will!

TONY EVANS

Consider it pure joy, my brothers, whenever you face trials of many kinds, because you know that the testing of your faith develops perseverance. Perseverance must finish its work so that you may be mature and complete, not lacking anything.

James 1:2-4

Our personal afflictions involve the living God; the only way in which Satan can persecute or afflict God is through attacking the people of God. The only way we can have personal victory in the midst of these flying arrows raining down on us is to call upon the Lord for help. It is His strength, supplied to us in our weakness, that makes victory after victory possible.

Edith Schaeffer

Sometimes God says "Wait" when we would rather move. Chuck Swindoll calls waiting the hardest discipline in the Christian life. I agree. That is why the psalmist says, "Be still before the LORD and wait patiently for him" (Psalm 37:7). God's guidance demands our obedience, even when it makes no sense to us. Sometimes God moves when we want to stay. Sometimes God says "Stay" when we would rather move on and get our life going again.

Ray Pritchard

Have we fallen? Are our lives shattered? God waits to pick us up. This does not minimize the challenge to share day by day in Christ's victory over sin. At the same time, however, there is His gentleness.

Francis A. Schaeffer

Do not be anxious about anything, but in everything, by prayer and petition, with thanksgiving, present your requests to God. And the peace of God, which transcends all understanding, will guard your hearts and your minds in Christ Jesus.

Philippians 4:6-7

Give ear to my words, O LORD,
    consider my sighing.
Listen to my cry for help, my King and my God,
    for to you I pray.
In the morning, O LORD,
    you hear my voice;
    in the morning I lay my requests before you
    and wait in expectation.

Psalm 5:1-3

Through our problems God can prove to the world how powerfully He provides for His people. The greater the need, the greater the testimony to God's grace, and often, by God's design, the greater the audience.

Tom Elliff

When you pass through the waters, I will be with you; and when you pass through the rivers, they will not sweep over you. When you walk through the fire, you will not be burned; the flames will not set you ablaze. For I am the LORD, your God.

Isaiah 43:2-3

God won't always shield you from persecution, but He will honor your integrity and give you strength to endure any trial that comes your way. Praise Him for His all-sufficient grace!

John MacArthur

Because God is infinite, He can care for us as if no one else were present in the universe. Because He is infinite, He never gets confused. And as Jesus so beautifully put it, the Good Shepherd knows His sheep by name.

Francis A. Schaeffer

If there is an all-powerful, loving God who is accomplishing His purposes behind the scenes, then we must never look at our present circumstances and conclude that what we see is all there is to reality. No matter what life looks like presently, no matter how much it appears that evil is winning, humans don't have the last word. God has the last word, and it is a word of hope, peace, and victory to those who love Him and who are walking in His will. But God's purposes take time to work out. So what we need while we wait for God's answer is patience and courage that comes from robust faith, and an absolute, flat-out refusal to believe that what we see is what we get. . . .

We assume that because we don't always see what God is doing, He is doing nothing. And because we see everything that evil is doing, we feel our fate is left dangling. We cannot afford to be naive. Our problem must be faced realistically and squarely. But when we are in a fearful situation, there is nothing that builds our confidence in God more than remembering His promises: "Do not be fainthearted or afraid; do not be terrified or give way to panic. . . . For the LORD your God is the one who goes with you to fight for you against your enemies to give you victory" (Deuteronomy 20:3-4).

Rebecca Manley Pippert

Life can knock the stuffing out of us. Testing and temptation can surface in different ways and different places in our lives. It can be a pathway to fearful, dark thoughts. It can be an excuse to enter the soggy marsh of self-pity. Or simply the quest to "get even" that starts out looking like justice. Testing is an individual matter. But God promises, "No temptation has overtaken you except such as is common to man; but God is faithful, who will not allow you to be tempted beyond what you are able, but with the temptation will also make the way of escape, that you may be able to bear it" (1 Corinthians 10:13 NKJV).

Nancie Carmichael

You were born again for courage, for bravery, for strength. God means for you to be an overcomer. If you are a believer, God has given you His Holy Spirit. You are not a loser. You were born again through Jesus Christ, and through the power of the Holy Spirit you can be victorious over the problems, struggles, and trials of life.

Ray Pritchard

As we remember what [God] has done in the past and cry out to Him for help in our present situation, our hearts are stirred to trust Him.

Ellen Banks Elwell

God is gracious to His children amid times of human sorrow. Ultimately He will do away with mourning and pain forever (Revelation 21:4). Rejoice in that promise, and be comforted by His wonderful grace!

John MacArthur

Pressing on in painful circumstances is the discipline of keeping our faith when everything not only goes wrong but becomes worse. It means holding onto the Lord during deep trials and asking Him to hold onto us when we feel weak in faith and hope.

Sheila Cragg

As brilliantly as the sun shines through some days, there are many days that it does not shine at all. Some days the clouds cover the mountains, and I must remind myself they are still there. And so I must continually remember that it is God's love that perfects, that makes the windows of our lives clear, that helps us see. There's much we don't understand now. All the more reason to accept grace and praise Him exactly from where we are.

Nancie Carmichael

Many times we start a new project believing that what we are doing is the will of God, and yet very often things do not work out as we planned. You took the job, and it didn't work out. You made the investment, and it didn't work out. You entered the relationship, and it didn't work out. You started school, and it didn't work out. You made a big decision, and it didn't work out. What do you do then? Our first reaction is usually to say, "Well, I must have been wrong; it couldn't have been the will of God."

I don't think that's the right answer.

Trouble does not necessarily mean you are out of God's will. It might mean that you are doing exactly what God wants you to do. Sometimes God sends trouble not as a judgment but as a sign that you are doing right. When Jesus was crucified, was He out of God's will? No. Yet His life ended in the midst of pain and suffering. No one was ever more in God's will than Jesus, but He was murdered by His enemies.

The fact that your life hasn't worked out exactly like you planned doesn't necessarily mean your decisions were wrong. Sometimes there are other factors at work.

Ray   Pritchard

See, I set before you today life and prosperity, death and destruction. For I command you today to love the LORD your God, to walk in his ways, and to keep his commands, decrees and laws.... Now choose life, so that you and your children may live and that you may love the LORD your God, listen to his voice, and hold fast to him. For the LORD is your life.

DEUTERONOMY 30:15-16, 19-20

True Measures of Success

WORLDLY PRAISE

IS ONE THING, BUT

THE PRAISE THAT

COMES FROM HEAVEN

IS QUITE ANOTHER.

Mike Mason

While the world is telling you to "reach for the stars" for your own personal satisfaction or materialistic gain, God is telling you to serve and work and live "with your whole heart" because He will ultimately judge your days and hours.

What sorts of achievements will elicit God's response of "Well done, good and faithful servant"? You'll discover that God's idea of success is a far cry from the one that's motivating the unbelieving world around you. ❦

When we stand before God's throne to give an account of how we used the time and talents He has given us, we may face a simple question: "What did I require of you? Did you act justly? Did you love mercy? Did you walk humbly with Me?" (Micah 6:8).

Lael F. Arrington

Prosperity is the reward of the righteous.

Proverbs 13:21

I am not the measure of my worth or my influence. God is. He is the one who knows the price tag I bear. He knows the price He paid to redeem me and make me His own. And He knows the investment He continues to make in me.

Roger C. Palms

Blessed is the man who does not walk in the counsel of the wicked or stand in the way of sinners or sit in the seat of mockers. But his delight is in the law of the LORD, and on his law he meditates day and night. He is like a tree planted by streams of water, which yields its fruit in season and whose leaf does not wither. Whatever he does prospers.

Psalms 1:1-3

When I was a college student, I used to mistake success for wisdom. If I did something well, such as getting good grades or getting a job other people would have wanted, I considered that I did it wisely. People tend to think that a family who gets a suitable house for a good price and a low mortgage has acted wisely. Success seems like wisdom because it reaches goals in the real world. Wisdom, if it is anything, is the ability to understand and act in the real world. But wisdom is more than that. Wisdom knows the right goals in the first place. I have learned that anything—even the wrong things—can be done successfully. The person who has wisdom knows what to aim at in the first place, not just how to hit a target.

Donna Morley

The brilliant light of a Roman candle streaks across the sky, evoking the pleasured exclamations of its audience. But it is quickly gone and forgotten, with no enduring impact. Will we settle for the applause of one great moment of public acclaim? Or will we seek the enduring influence that only comes when one is willing to develop the discipline of a quiet time and a quiet place—to regularly and consistently take time to sit at our Savior's feet to learn from Him?

Tom Elliff

Be careful to obey all the law my servant Moses gave you; do not
turn from it to the right or to the left, that you may be successful
wherever you go.

Joshua 1:7

Blessed are all who fear the LORD, who walk in his ways. You will
eat the fruit of your labor; blessings and prosperity will be yours.

Psalms 128:1-2

Every individual has a basic desire for joy, and it seems that all
other desires flow from there and directly or indirectly serve that
most basic need. People consume certain foods and beverages
because they get enjoyment from them. People seek to gain money
and material possessions because they believe those things will
bring joy. Most people seek prestige, power, and success because
they think those will also bring joy. But that kind of enjoyment is
temporary and disappointing. Real and lasting joy comes only as
believers, by faith through grace, trust Jesus Christ as Lord and
Savior and appropriate the truths of His kingdom.

John MacArthur

He who trusts in the LORD will prosper.

Proverbs 28:25

May I never boast except in the cross of our Lord Jesus Christ, through which the world has been crucified to me, and I to the world.

Galatians 6:14

Here is the essence of the covenant: God came, He called, and He clothed. And He has been doing the same down through the ages. He comes to us, He calls us to Himself, and He clothes us with the righteousness of Christ. He relates to us not on the basis of our performance, but on the basis of His provision.

Susan Hunt

"Have faith in the LORD your God and you will be upheld; have faith in his prophets and you will be successful."

2 Chronicles 20:20

Are you a Phil Beta Kappa, an All-American, Miss America, listed in *Who's Who,* voted "Most Likely to Succeed," or in the blue book of society? If you answered yes to any or all of these questions, I have good news for you. God can still use you, though He is going to have a little more difficulty doing it.

But if, on the other hand, you have done or achieved none of the things the world prizes so highly, God delights to use you. If you have never won anything but the booby prize, God desires to get glory through you. As a matter of fact, He prefers to use ordinary people. . . .

Do you consider yourself a nobody? Well, with God everybody is a somebody. He is looking for someone like you. Your name may not be mentioned much down here, but God wants you to make headlines in heaven.

Adrian Rogers

Are you a winner? You need only to begin your pilgrimage at the cross and, trusting God's grace through life's ups and downs, persevere in faith till your journey's end.

Cheryl V. Ford

Each person's life, although no longer perfect, has inestimable value. We don't have to earn worth; we are each one precious. God has created us to have a relationship with Himself—with a future that transcends the seen world and death. This reality is contrary to today's materialistic evaluation of individual persons, their worth, and their everyday lives.

Susan Schaeffer Macaulay

*T*hough these lines from "If," a poem by Rudyard Kipling, are not avowedly Christian, they contain some biblical wisdom:

> If you can dream—and not make dreams your master;
> If you can think—and not make thoughts your aim;
> If you can meet with Triumph and Disaster
> And treat those two imposters just the same . . .

Then, says Kipling eventually, "you'll be a Man, my son!" . . . Kipling tells us that the mature person will be able to imagine new possibilities, yet without losing touch with reality; he will be able to conceptualize and argue and debate, yet without becoming a doctrinaire theorist; and beyond that, he will view any present success and any present collapse of his projects as delusive to a degree, looking like what they are not, and therefore he will take them in stride as simply episodes in the unfolding tapestry of a purposeful life. . . . A moment of conscious triumph makes one feel that after this nothing will really matter; a moment of realized disaster makes one feel that this is the end of everything. But neither feeling is realistic, for neither event is really what it is felt to be. The circumstances of triumph will not last, and the moment of triumph will sooner or later give way to moments of disappointment, strain, frustration, and grief, while the circumstances of disaster will prove to have in them seeds of recovery and new hope. Life in this world under God's providence is like that; it always has been and always will be; it is so in the Bible, and it remains so as the twentieth century gives way to the twenty-first. The mature person, who is mentally and emotionally an adult, as distinct from a child, knows this and does not forget it.

J. I. PACKER

"For we are laborers together with God" (1 Corinthians 3:9 KJV): There is the great secret of success. Work with all your might, but trust not the least in your work. Pray with all your might for the blessing of God; but work at the same time, with all diligence, with all patience, with all perseverance. Pray and then work. Work and pray. And still again pray and then work. And so on all the days of your life. The result will surely be abundant blessing. . . . Speak also for the Lord, as if everything depended on your exertions. Yet trust not the least in your exertions, but in the Lord, who alone can cause your efforts to be made effectual, to the benefit of your fellow-men or fellow-believers.

George Muller

"His master replied, 'Well done, good and faithful servant! You have been faithful with a few things; I will put you in charge of many things. Come and share your master's happiness!'"

Matthew 25:21

And the LORD was with him; he was successful in whatever he undertook.

2 Kings 18:7

beyond today

When we make ourselves or others our focus, we will lose. When God is the center, we win—no matter what happens to us.

Roger C. Palms

Whoever trusts in his riches will fall, but the righteous will thrive like a green leaf.

Proverbs 11:28

Even though we live, work, study, and play in this world, we are not supposed to reflect its values and attitudes (John 17:15-16, 18; 1 John 2:15). Because of who we are, we must influence the world toward salvation and God's standards of righteousness, not toward more selfishness, amorality, and materialism. We are to be in the world but not of the world.

John MacArthur

The LORD was with Joseph and he prospered.

Genesis 39:2

Blessed are they whose ways are blameless, who walk according to the law of the LORD.

Psalm 119:1

There was a girl who was supposed to make cakes in the Les Melezes kitchen, and she got all messed up until she had nothing but a mess of goo. It seemed as though there was nothing to do but throw the mess out. . . . But, by adding an extra ingredient, Edith was able to make it into the most marvelous noodles you have tasted in your life.

We often do this with our lives, and then perhaps we won't be the cakes we could have been. But if we give ourselves into the hands of the Lord, He can very much reshape us to be something other than we would have been, but something with both usefulness and beauty.

Francis A. Schaeffer

A career for status or success or power, a high salary, or a have-it-all lifestyle are the biblical "mammon." These are the values of the world. Other places in Scripture warn us that much effort for such goals leads to a result that is like straw, which blows away in the wind, as far as God is concerned. What will remain at life's end? What is precious to God?

Susan Schaeffer Macaulay

CHAPTER TWELVE

Follow my example, as I follow

the example of Christ.

1 CORINTHIANS 11:1

beyond
today

Servant Leadership

YOU ARE EXCEPTIONAL.
GOD HAS CREATED
NO ONE EXACTLY LIKE
YOU. YOUR LIFE CAN
HAVE A GODLY IMPACT
ON OTHER PEOPLE,
EVEN IF YOU DON'T
SEE THAT IMPACT
DURING YOUR LIFETIME.

Richard L. Ganz

beyond
   today

Whether or not you see yourself as a leader,

someone somewhere is looking up to you—a child, a friend, a

coworker. As a believer, you're light in this sin-darkened world.

How will you use the gifts God has given you, a unique individ-

ual, to serve and to lead?

Christians do not need to be in the majority in order to influence society.

Francis A. Schaeffer

Before I was born the LORD called me; from my birth he has made mention of my name. . . . He said to me, "You are my servant, Israel, in whom I will display my splendor."

Isaiah 49: 1, 3

God makes leaders by taking people with the right raw material, putting them through the right experiences, and teaching them the right lessons. . . .

Just as God transformed Peter from a brash and impulsive fisherman into a powerful instrument for His glory, so He can transform everyone who is yielded to Him.

You will never be an apostle, but you can have the same depth of character and can know the same joy of serving Christ that Peter knew. There's no higher calling in the world than to be an instrument of God's grace. Peter was faithful to that calling. May you be faithful too!

John MacArthur

As we look to Jesus as a guide to what leadership or headship means, we know that although He encourages our individuality, creativity, and choices, He never swerves from the moral absolutes and truth that are the backbone of life. These give strength, shape, structure, and stability. He also always follows "the rules" He gives us to obey—rules that enable goodness, rightness, truth, love, and life.

Susan Schaeffer Macaulay

Effective business leaders know the importance of clarifying their core commitments—excellence, integrity, service, and so on. But this awareness of core commitments is sadly lacking (and is desperately needed) in our homes, families, and nation. Many people have little idea what their core commitments really are and don't understand the significance of those commitments. If you are a Christian, you are committed to Jesus Christ.

Richard L. Ganz

It was he who gave some to be apostles, some to be prophets, some to be evangelists, and some to be pastors and teachers, to prepare God's people for works of service, so that the body of Christ may be built up.

Ephesians 4:11-12

God uses our experiences to mold us into more effective Christians and leaders. . . . Submission, restraint, humility, sacrifice, and love should be characteristic of every believer—no matter what role he or she has within the body of Christ. I pray they are characteristic of your life and that you will constantly seek to grow in those graces as God continues His work in you.

John MacArthur

Don't let anyone look down on you because you are young, but set an example for the believers in speech, in life, in love, in faith and in purity.

1 Timothy 4:12

None of us are ready for leadership until we come to the place before the Lord where we are really ready for His will—regardless of what it is.

Francis A. Schaeffer

We live in a world where spiritual power is still the real power behind what happens, and we need to be prepared to operate in the sphere of the power of God under His divine leadership.

Timothy M. Warner

*I*t's been said that no one likes playing second fiddle, but that wasn't Andrew's perspective at all. Growing up in the shadow of an aggressive, outspoken brother like Peter would be a challenge for anyone. Even in the biblical record Andrew is known as "Simon Peter's brother" (John 1:40). Yet when Andrew met Jesus, his first response was to tell Peter, knowing full well that once Peter became a disciple, he probably would run the group. But Andrew was a truly humble man who was more concerned about bringing people to Christ than about who was in charge. . . .

Andrew symbolizes all those humble, faithful, and courageous Christians who labor behind the scenes. They're the backbone of every ministry and the ones on whom every leader depends. You might never be a prominent leader like Peter, but you can be a faithful, courageous servant like Andrew.

JOHN MACARTHUR

Only the Holy Spirit can create in us the kind of love towards our Savior that will overflow in imaginative sympathy and practical helpfulness towards His people. Unless the Spirit is training us in love, we are not fit persons to go to college or a training class to learn the know-how of particular branches of Christian work. Gifted leaders who are self-centered and loveless are a blight in the church rather than a blessing.

J. I. Packer

If anyone sets his heart on being an overseer, he desires a noble task. Now the overseer must be above reproach, the husband of but one wife, temperate, self-controlled, respectable, hospitable, able to teach, not given to drunkenness, not violent but gentle, not quarrelsome, not a lover of money. He must manage his own family well and see that his children obey him with proper respect. . . . He must also have a good reputation with outsiders, so that he will not fall into disgrace and into the devil's trap. Deacons, likewise, are to be men worthy of respect, sincere, not indulging in much wine, and not pursuing dishonest gain. They must keep hold of the deep truths of the faith with a clear conscience.

1 Timothy 3:1-9

Mature people speak up and insist on being heard. Mature people, in turn, listen and are willing to give in if that is right. Such individuals can either lead or follow. They don't have to be the one in charge. They are glad to cooperate or stay behind the scenes.

Susan Schaeffer Macaulay

"Be strong and courageous, because you will lead these people to inherit the land I swore to their forefathers to give them. Be strong and very courageous. Be careful to obey all the law. . . . Be strong and courageous. Do not be terrified; do not be discouraged, for the LORD your God will be with you wherever you go."

Joshua 1:6-7, 9

God is saying, "If you want to be effective, you must think about your conduct. What will be the consequences of your behavior? Where will your current choices ultimately take you?"

Tom Elliff

Where are the leaders who inspire public opinion, who influence their peers, encourage them not to follow their feelings, but to trust God and follow their conscience? Our children need to be inspired by people like Martin Luther. A monk charged with

"heresy," he stood up against the false teachings of the pope and the entire Catholic church: "I am bound by the Scripture I have quoted, and my conscience is captive to the Word of God." . . . This is the kind of leadership our children need to see—leadership of conscience held "captive to the Word of God." Consistently, graciously, faithfully, we need to live before them and lead according to conscience against the progressive cultural flow.

Lael F. Arrington

One of the most striking evidences of sinful human nature lies in the universal propensity for downward drift. In other words, it takes thought, resolve, energy, and effort to bring about reform. In the grace of God, sometimes human beings display such virtues. . . . Genuine reformation and revival have never occurred in the church apart from leaders for whom devotion to God is of paramount importance.

D. A. Carson

The Lord's servant must not quarrel; instead, he must be kind to everyone, able to teach, not resentful. Those who oppose him he must gently instruct, in the hope that God will grant them repentance leading them to a knowledge of the truth.

2 Timothy 2:24-25

Reaching your potential requires commitment. Exceptional people who may do exceptional things usually put a great deal of effort and practice into achieving specific goals. Godly men and women, for example, dedicate themselves to knowing God and His Word.

Richard L. Ganz

We have different gifts, according to the grace given us. If a man's gift is prophesying, let him use it in proportion to his faith. If it is serving, let him serve; if it is teaching, let him teach; if it is encouraging, let him encourage; if it is contributing to the needs of others, let him give generously; if it is leadership, let him govern diligently.

Romans 12:6-8

Remember your leaders, who spoke the word of God to you. Consider the outcome of their way of life and imitate their faith. . . . Obey your leaders and submit to their authority. They keep watch over you as men who must give an account. Obey them so that their work will be a joy.

Hebrews 13:7, 17

Jesus assures us that His authority is considerate and thoughtful. It is "humble" and "gentle." This means that He is aware of the other person; He is other-centered. Humility is an attitude we must work toward; we don't find it easy. Then if we are wise, we'll know that we don't really know much either, as we recognize our limitations. . . . This is the amazing model for leadership in the home, church, and society.

Susan Schaeffer Macaulay

The word of the LORD came to me, saying, "Before I formed you in the womb I knew you, before you were born I set you apart; I appointed you as a prophet to the nations."

Jeremiah 1:4-5

Some Christians have a zeal that prompts them to run ahead of the Holy Spirit. If that's true of you, be thankful for your zeal, but also be careful to allow the Spirit to govern what you do and say. However, if you've slipped into spiritual complacency and your life isn't much of a threat to Satan's kingdom, you need to repent and become more zealous for the Lord!

John MacArthur

CHAPTER THIRTEEN

No eye has seen, no ear has heard,

no mind has conceived what God has

prepared for those who love him.

1   CORINTHIANS   2 : 9

Now and Forever

WE MUST LIVE

BELIEVING GOD IS

KING AND HIS

KINDOM IS NOW

AND IS COMING!

LET US BELIEVE IT.

LET US PROCLAIM

TOGETHER, "THINE

IS THE KINDOM."

R. Kent Hughes

beyond
today

When you accepted Christ,

you stepped right into your future—by being born into a kingdom

that never ends, the kingdom of God. The Bible describes the possi-

bilities of your life right now as "abundant" and as a time for being

transformed more and more into the likeness of Christ. God's Word

also points to your future in heaven, where you'll see Christ face to

face and share in His glory.

Talk about great expectations! As a Christian, you've got the

greatest. 🦋

It would be incorrect for us to think that everlasting life begins only when our bodies die. For those who trust Christ as Savior, everlasting life begins *immediately*, giving us a portfolio of riches.

Ellen Banks Elwell

Even to your old age and gray hairs I am he, I am he who will sustain you. I have made you and I will carry you; I will sustain you and I will rescue you.

Isaiah 46:4

For the Lord himself will come down from heaven, with a loud command, with the voice of the archangel and with the trumpet call of God, and the dead in Christ will rise first. After that, we who are still alive and are left will be caught up together with them in the clouds to meet the Lord in the air. And so we will be with the Lord forever. Therefore encourage each other with these words.

1 Thessalonians 4:16-18

The coming advent of the kingdom of God is no impossibility. Let no one call it a utopia. It is as sure as any established fact of history. In it our dreams will come true!

R. Kent Hughes

beyond today

I am like an olive tree flourishing in the house of God; I trust in God's unfailing love for ever and ever.

Psalm 52:8

For most of us eternity seems, well, so far ahead. And it seems like we will never get there. So we are tempted to forget the hereafter and just focus on the here and now. But are we doing anything that will affect the future?

Donna Morley

"Behold, I will create new heavens and a new earth. The former things will not be remembered, nor will they come to mind. But be glad and rejoice forever in what I will create, for I will create Jerusalem to be a delight and its people a joy."

Isaiah 65:17

Do not let your hearts be troubled. Trust in God; trust also in me. In my Father's house are many rooms; if it were not so, I would have told you. I am going there to prepare a place for you. And if I go and prepare a place for you, I will come back and take you to be with me that you also may be where I am.

John 14:1-3

For the world, Christ's future appearance will mean judgment. But to those who have come to God through Him, it will be a time of rest with God.

Francis A. Schaeffer

God exalted him to the highest place and gave him the name that is above every name, that at the name of Jesus every knee should bow, in heaven and on earth and under the earth, and every tongue confess that Jesus Christ is Lord, to the glory of God the Father.

Philippians 2:9-11

In the future Jesus will return as Prince of Peace to establish a kingdom that will usher us into an eternal age of peace. In the meantime He reigns over the hearts of all who love Him. Let His peace reign in your heart today!

John MacArthur

There is much truth in the statement, "The way you live is the way you die." What will we focus on toward the end of our lives? It all depends on what we focus on now.

Donna Morley

Heaven is where holiness, fellowship with God, joy, peace, love, and all other virtues are realized in utter perfection, but we experience all those things—at least partially—even now. The Holy Spirit is producing in us the fruit of "love, joy, peace, patience, kindness, goodness, faithfulness, gentleness, self-control" (Galatians 5:22-23). Again, those are the same traits that characterize heaven. Moreover, we have the life of God in us and the rule of God over us. We know joy, peace, love, goodness, and blessing. We have become part of a new family, a new kind of community. We have left the kingdom of darkness for the kingdom of light. We are no longer under the dominion of Satan but the dominion of God in Christ. . . .

We can live in the glow of heaven's glory here and now, with our hearts already in heaven. This is to say that the Christian life is meant to be like heaven on earth. Believers regularly taste the sweetness of the same heaven to which someday we will go to dwell forever. Praising and loving God with all your being, adoring and obeying Christ, pursuing holiness, cherishing fellowship with other saints—those are the elements of heavenly life we can begin to taste in this world. Those same pursuits and privileges will occupy us forever, but we can begin to practice them even now.

JOHN MACARTHUR

If you have believed on Jesus as your Savior, go ahead and pull back the curtain. Dare to look ahead. Look ahead to the day when your body will be resurrected, when with your resurrected eyes you will see the glories of the redeemed, restored creation. Look ahead to the day when, free in your glorified state from the very presence of sin, you will live with your Lord forever.

Francis A. Schaeffer

Listen, I tell you a mystery: We will not all sleep, but we will all be changed—in a flash, in the twinkling of an eye, at the last trumpet. For the trumpet will sound, the dead will be raised imperishable, and we will be changed.

1 Corinthians 15:51-52

Whatsoever the Lord takes in hand He will accomplish; hence past mercies are guarantees for the future, and admirable reasons for continuing to cry unto Him.

C. H. Spurgeon

Heaven is . . . a place, a real place, where the people of God go after they die. It is God's home.

John MacArthur

But encourage one another daily, as long as it is called Today, so that none of you may be hardened by sin's deceitfulness. We have come to share in Christ if we hold firmly till the end the confidence we had at first.

Hebrews 3:13-14

What anticipation we feel for a day yet to come when we will experience *ultimate* security—sharing communion together with Christ in heaven!

Ellen Banks Elwell

If you are a Christian, heaven is your future home for all eternity. It is where all things are made new.

John MacArthur

It is easy to forget that becoming a Christian is only the beginning. The journey of a thousand miles begins with the first step, but the purpose of the first step is the whole journey. It is not the other way around.

Os Guinness

He will swallow up death forever. The Sovereign LORD will wipe away the tears from all faces; he will remove the disgrace of his people from all the earth. The LORD has spoken.

Isaiah 25:8

Our lives are so brief that we cannot afford to live carelessly or aimlessly. The proper attitude that believers are instructed to have is: "If it is the Lord's will, we will live to do this or that." Those may also be words that we speak to others, but most important, they need to be words that our hearts speak to God. We do this by spending time daily, regularly, praying and asking God that His will be done in our lives.

Ellen Banks Elwell

Seek first his kingdom and his righteousness, and all these things will be given to you as well. Therefore do not worry about tomorrow, for tomorrow will worry about itself.

Matthew 6:33-34

In keeping with his promise we are looking forward to a new heaven and a new earth, the home of righteousness.

2 Peter 3:13

beyond
today

We'll grow in godliness as we keep putting our complete trust in the One who knows our future. He desires that we have peace about tomorrow, for He is our future and will take care of all our tomorrows.

Sheila Cragg

Amidst all the evidence of cultural decline, however, I believe there is great hope for the future! Because, as the pain increases, people's hearts become open to the Gospel. Misguided public policies and people's lives are crashing into the wall of reality, and many are ready to admit failure and seek new solutions. This means we have a great open door to share the Gospel and to bring Christian influence to bear on our culture.

Lael F. Arrington

[God] does not change. He will be tomorrow as He was yesterday. We can depend on Him to be faithful, reliable, trustworthy. He has said He understands us. We are told that the promises He made centuries ago are just as true today—not just true in the academic sense of truth, but true to you and me personally. His truth makes a difference in our present lives, as well as to our part and place in eternity.

Edith Schaeffer

O God, have mercy. Let me live today in such a way that I may have no regrets when I come to tomorrow. Let me lay a firm foundation for eternity, by Your grace and mercy. In the holy name of Christ, amen.

Raymond C. Ortlund, Jr.

Christ knew the preciousness of time. He knew of the glory that soon awaited Him in heaven, which made His time on earth that much more crucial. Now was the time to plant seed, before "night is coming, when no man can work" (John 9:4). Now was the time to bring words of compassion, truth, and life—to bring kindness and healing.

Life, minute by minute, goes by only once, and I have learned only too well that when I misspend time, I can never get it back. Time moves relentlessly like the hands of a clock. All too quickly will my abilities to serve God and others evaporate into thin air.

Donna Morley

Thank the Lord for His gracious care in bringing you safely this far. Thank Him that He will also continue to work in your behalf throughout the remainder of your life's pilgrimage. Reaffirm your trust in His faithfulness.

Cheryl V. Ford

beyond
today

uotations are taken from the Bible and from the following Crossway books:

Arrington, Lael F., *Worldproofing Your Kids*
Arthur, William, quoted in *Into His Presence*
Boice, James Montgomery and Philip Graham Ryken, *The Heart of the Cross*
Carmichael, Nancie, *Desperate for God*
_____, *Your Life, God's Home*
Carson, D. A., *For the Love of God,* Vol. 2
Cook, Charles A., quoted in *Into His Presence*
Cragg, Sheila, *A Woman's Journey Toward Holiness*
_____, *A Woman's Pilgrimage of Faith*
_____, *A Woman's Walk with God*
Elliff, Tom, *A Passion for Prayer*
Elwell, Ellen Banks, *Quiet Moments of Encouragement for Moms*
_____, *Quiet Moments of Faith for Moms*
_____, *Quiet Moments of Hope for Moms*
_____, *Quiet Moments of Wisdom for Moms*
Evans, Debra, *The Christian Woman's Guide to Sexuality*
Evans, Tony, *No More Excuses*
_____, *Time to Get Serious*
Ford, Cheryl V., *The Pilgrim's Progress Devotional*
Ganz, Richard L., *The Secret of Self-Control*
Guinness, Os, *God in the Dark*
Haney, David, *A Living Hope*
Hughes, R. Kent, *Abba Father*
_____, *Disciplines of a Godly Man*
_____, *Disciplines of Grace*
Hunt, Susan, *By Design*
_____, *The True Woman*
Lawson, Steven, *Faith Under Fire*
_____, *Final Call*
Lloyd-Jones, Martyn, *The Cross*
_____, *Revival*
MacArthur, John, *Drawing Near*
_____, *Forgiveness*
_____, *The Glory of Heaven*

_____, *In the Footsteps of Faith*

_____, *Nothing but the Truth*

_____, *The Pillars of Christian Character*

_____, *The Power of Integrity*

_____, *The Second Coming*

Macaulay, Susan Schaeffer, *For the Family's Sake*

MacLaren, Alexander, quoted in *Into His Presence*

Mason, Mike, *The Gospel According to Job*

Meyer, F. B., quoted in *Into His Presence*

Miller, J. R., quoted in *Into His Presence*

Morley, Donna, *Choices That Lead to Godliness*

Muller, George, quoted in *Into His Presence*

Olford, Stephen F., *Not I but Christ*

_____, *The Way of Holiness*

Ortlund, Jr., Raymond C., *A Passion for God*

Owens, Daniel, *Sharing Christ When You Feel You Can't*

The Oxford Dictionary of Quotations

Packer, J. I., *Growing in Christ*

_____, *Life in the Spirit*

_____, *A Passion for Faithfulness*

_____, *A Quest for Godliness*

Palms, Roger C., *An Unexpected Hope*

Ryken, Philip Graham, *Courage to Stand*

_____, *Discovering God in Stories from the Bible*

Piper, John, *A Hunger for God*

Pippert, Rebecca Manley, *A Heart Like His*

Pritchard, Ray, *Man of Honor*

_____, *The Road Best Traveled*

_____, *What a Christian Believes*

Rogers, Adrian, *The Power of His Presence*

Schaeffer, Edith, *The Art of Life*

_____, *The Life of Prayer*

Schaeffer, Francis A., *The Finished Work of Christ*

_____, *How Should We Then Live?*

_____, *Letters of Francis A. Schaeffer*

Spurgeon, C. H., quoted in *Into His Presence*

Warner, Timothy M., *Spiritual Warfare*